Immanuel God with us

A spiritual focus for personal or group use

A 31-DAY ADVENT GUIDE

ANNE LE TISSIER

Published 2006 by CWR, Waverley Abbey House, Waverley Lane, Farnham, Surrey GU9 8EP, England.

See back of book for list of National Distributors.

Concept development, editing, design and production by CWR

Cover image: Digital Vision

Printed in Finland by WS Bookwell

ISBN-13: 978-1-85345-390-8
ISBN-10: 1-85345-390-0

Contents

Introduction

Engaging with Immanuel, God with us – past, present and future

I was delighted when CWR approached me to write their third Advent book in the *Cover to Cover* series, but signing the contract culminated in a good degree of soul-searching as I contemplated what Advent means to me and what, if any, significance it has in my life.

Having grappled with those questions personally, I then set out to establish what, if any, meaning and significance it held for Christians from various denominations and backgrounds. A few folk intimated that Advent was a helpful period for spiritual growth while others admitted that it didn't have any significance in their lives. Many replied that while they yearned for a meaningful time of spiritual reflection, more often than not it became a panic-ridden, financially daunting, stress-filled period of frantic activity. One amusing but poignant response read as follows:

> Advent means … the run up to Christmas, and that means a whole host of things. It's a funny thought, Advent, because it's the beginning; the beginning of the end, the beginning of opening 'Pandora's Box'. Oh yes, and Christmas is coming. Christmas will be here in four weeks – FOUR WEEKS! And off comes the lid and out come all the fears and terrors of having to cope/buy/organise/invite/survive…
>
> (Mrs Pauline Cooper, quoted with permission)

As commercial hype and secularisation increasingly push Christ out of Christmas preparations, we all have a decision to make:

Will we

1. gripe and grumble over the commercial intrusion, harking back to the good old days when the focus of Advent and Christmas at least appeared to remain on Christ;
2. give in to the rat-race and temporarily lose sight of what we really believe and celebrate; or
3. provide a realistic, tangible, tempting alternative to the world as we renew the significance of *Immanuel* through our personal walk with Jesus?

God came to be with us in human form; He comes to us today through the indwelling of the Holy Spirit; and Jesus is coming again as King and Lord of lords. The angels were ecstatic at His arrival on earth, as were Simeon and Anna. His birth stirred shepherds to leave their flocks, and Magi to travel hundreds of miles to offer their precious gifts. His life of love attracted men and women to meet His human needs and serve God's kingdom purposes. This Immanuel longs to have an impact on our lives; that His presence may empower our lifestyles and thinking, and so protect our faith from being hijacked by frenzied 'winter-fest mania'.

The prophets prepared Israel to receive their future Saviour, the angel Gabriel prepared Mary for His birth, John the Baptist prepared His contemporaries to meet Him as a man and Jesus prepared His disciples to make Him known to the world. The baton has now been passed on to us – to prepare ourselves and our own generation to meet Immanuel.

Whether your experience embraces this season wholeheartedly or casts it off as irrelevant religiosity, I invite you to join with me for a month of Advent reflections; a period in which we may strengthen our resolve to live with the Advent message that Jesus came, Jesus comes and Jesus is coming again.

How To Use *Immanuel: God with us*

For personal use

This book has been written as a 31-day reflection for the month of December, each day requiring about fifteen minutes of your time. The key to getting the most out of any form of devotion, however, is to shut out other distractions and prayerfully absorb God's living Word. When we're busy and tired it's easy to merely read with our eyes, but I trust that we'll consider and pray the words from our hearts. It may also be helpful to keep a notepad handy to write down any thoughts, questions or prayer points arising each day.

For group use

Midweek home groups or seasonal Advent groups may also like to use this book. Each member, however, would need to commit to the material personally on a day-to-day basis and then use the 'Coming Together' sections for group meetings once a week. The role of the group leader would simply be encouraging discussion of the points raised, organising words and music for the suggested worship song and providing a suitable setting for quiet reflection.

Postcript

One of my nostalgic childhood memories includes the seasonal Advent calendar. I can still feel the excitement of running downstairs each morning, trying to guess what the picture might be behind the little cardboard door. Joshua, aged eight, however, recently spotted the Advent questionnaire I'd sent to his granny and asked if he could fill one out too. After some thought he responded as follows: 'The significance of Advent: I have chocolate every day from the Advent calendar!' (quoted with permission).

So, for those of us who still enjoy them, I've incorporated a variation of both the picture and chocolate calendars within this book. Here, we can reflect on an image of our lives or circumstances, asking as we do so for the Spirit to speak to our soul while inwardly digesting the meaningful implication of a morsel of God's Word.

Anne Le Tissier
2006

WEEK ONE

Advent: An Arrival or Coming

1 DEC

Advent: A commercialised tradition?

The means of remembering past events may well birth activities that, over time, we call traditions – the handing down from generation to generation of the same customs, beliefs, etc.[1] In fact, look up the word 'Advent' in any Bible concordance and it won't appear because it's a human custom. So is it right as Christians, to observe Advent without specific scriptural mandate to do so?

Scriptural foundations...
Read Exodus 12:14–42

God gave the Israelites detailed instructions on how to commemorate the day He rescued them from Egypt. Thus, God ordained it was good to remember, give thanks and celebrate how He released them from slavery. Fourteen hundred years later, however, Paul wrote concerning such traditions, '...do not let anyone judge you by what you eat or drink, or with regard to a religious festival ... These are a shadow of the things that were to come; the reality, however, is found in Christ' (Col. 2:16–17).

Jesus wasn't born into the world to abolish the Law and its inherent traditions, rather He came to fulfil them (Matt. 5:17). And so, during His final meal with the disciples, the annual Passover feast, 'he took bread, gave thanks and broke it, and gave it to them, saying, "This is my body given for you; do this in remembrance of me"' (Luke 22:19). Holy days and feasts were a mere shadow of the reality of a religion based upon relationship with God through Christ. Nevertheless, Jesus ordained that it is good to remember, give thanks and celebrate how God released the world from slavery to sin; a process involving His birth, death, resurrection and future return.

...on which we build

Advent, by Western Church tradition, begins on the fourth Sunday before Christmas Day and ends on 24 December. Furthermore, it didn't exist until introduced by Pope Gregory in the sixth century, since which time the traditional use of carols, candles, colour and corporate worship have augmented this festive season. But as some may condemn certain Church traditions as irrelevant religiosity, it's helpful to know what you and I feel personally concerning the Advent season.

This has become increasingly important as Christmas and its preceding preparations have developed into as much a secular celebration as a Christian one; commercial activity retailing extortionate sums of money for parties, presents, decorations, food and drink, further encouraged by adverts to the tune of, 'indulge yourself – it's Christmas'.

So, whatever our experience or opinion of Advent tradition, let's primarily seek to uphold, as at any time of the year, a sustainable focus on thanksgiving and praise to God.

Advent Calendar

For digestion: 'See to it that no-one takes you captive through hollow and deceptive philosophy, which depends on human tradition and the basic principles of this world rather than on Christ' (Col. 2:8).
For reflection: Picture your usual Advent activities: where is Christ – at the centre or at the periphery?

Consider or discuss

In the Introduction I mentioned my Advent questionnaire. Now it's your turn to complete it – your initial thoughts in just one sentence for each question:

- What does Advent mean to you?
- What significance (if any) does Advent have for you?

Prayer
Forgive me, Lord, when my heart has not been in worship, when I've honoured you with my lips but not my lifestyle. Please help me through this Advent season to build up my most holy faith. Amen.

Pray for others
Pray for the 10,000 people groups who do not know the nature of Christ who came to earth;[2] those for whom Advent is unheard of (possibly close to a quarter of the world's population), and for organisations dedicated to reaching them with the gospel.

2 DEC

Advent past and future

With both religious and commercial tradition competing for our attention at this festive time of year, it may be helpful to define the word from which this season takes it name:

> advent – an arrival or coming, esp. one which is awaited [from Latin *adventus*].[3]

Scriptural foundations...
Read Revelation 1:4–8

The eternality of God Almighty is encompassed in John's use of a striking title, '… who is, and who was, and who is to come … the Alpha and the Omega' (Rev. 1:4,8). But snuck in between these bookends of divine completeness we read of Jesus, 'the faithful witness' (v.5).

To be a genuine, faithful witness one has to have first-hand evidence of the situation under review, so Jesus could not testify to God's endless dominion if He'd only seen just a part of it. Thus, if our Advent focus tends toward His Bethlehem birth we may overlook the significant fact that He did not come abruptly into being, circa 3 BC.

Although Jesus was only on earth for thirty-three years, He was with God from the beginning (John 1:1–2) and thus, before the creation of the world (Gen. 1:1). He now sits at God's right hand in heaven (Heb. 1:3) and will one day return to reign as eternal King of kings (Rev. 11:15).

...on which we build

The original definition of *advent* highlights the dual theme of traditional Advent worship; the season in which we prepare to give thanks for the *arrival* of the long-awaited Messiah, coupled with the anticipation of His *coming* again as King.

Nevertheless, many of the heart-warming traditions surrounding nativity imagery focus our attention on a very short period in the past, while glossing over, or forgetting completely, the future to which that period of history alludes. Perhaps that's why many non-believers feel comfortable celebrating the traditional joy of the Christmas story, provided they're not challenged by its potential implications. Thus we can see how tradition for tradition's sake without meaningful application for the present and relevance for the future, is as perilous as keeping a time-bomb!

This week, as we continue to unpack the potential spiritual stimuli of Advent, let's ask God to broaden our minds to His far bigger picture and purpose for our world; to breathe new life into our busy December preparations. And let's give thanks that to do so, we have help in abundance through the living reality of relationship with God.

Advent Calendar

For digestion: 'Jesus Christ is the same yesterday and today and for ever' (Heb. 13:8).

For reflection: Open the door of your heart and peep inside. What sentiments override your Advent focus; the joy of the Bethlehem story, the stress of preparing for Christmas or the anticipation of Christ's return?

Consider or discuss

Bring to mind any Advent traditions you maintain in your home:

- What proportion prepares people's hearts to celebrate Christ's arrival as a baby, compared with those that anticipate His coming again?

- Do you maintain any traditions that lack a true Advent significance? If so, how might you make them more meaningful to yourself, your children, your non-believing family and friends, and/or people who may otherwise benefit from the time and money you spend in maintaining them?

Prayer

King of creation, I praise You, for You are worthy of my praise.

King in the manger, I remember with heartfelt thanksgiving Your willingness to leave the rich glory of heaven that I might meet You in the Person of Jesus.

King of the cross, words seem inadequate to thank You for restoring intimate relationship with my heavenly Father.

King, Immanuel, God with us, I thank You for Your Spirit who meets with me today.

King of kings, Lord of lords, I praise You, for You are worthy of my praise;

I cannot wait until I see You face to face.

Pray for others

Pray for organisations such as Tearfund and The Leprosy Mission[4] for the success of their seasonal catalogues selling cards and gifts promoting cottage industry in developing countries, thus helping alleviate poverty while supplementing income for their charitable work and mission.

3 DEC

Advent 'arrival'

We're only just into December, but tinsel-draped window displays are already crammed with potential gifts, supermarkets overflow with festive food and decorative lights attract young and old to shopping centres, seafronts and even to private residences.

I wonder how many people have forgotten the reason why.

Scriptural foundations...
Read Isaiah 9:1–7

God armed His people with power to conquer Canaan's inhabitants; He provided them with homes in the bountiful promised land and chose to dwell among them within the magnificent Temple. But they grew complacent with His protective presence, they tired of saying thank you for His daily provision, they compromised the holy pattern of sacrifice and worship, misapplying their means of mercy as a liberal licence to sin. Over and over again, God's prophets warned Israel of its impending doom but they would not confess their wayward behaviour until there was no turning back from judgment.

Today, however, we read how Isaiah brought hope into the nation's eventual repentant despair. God promised to rescue His people from exile. Moreover, He would send to them the Messiah who would save them from their sins once for all – and not just Israel, but the entire world.

Seven hundred years later the Saviour arrived – a vulnerable human baby.

...on which we build
In restoring the significance of Advent to our commercialised society, we must first consider the 'arrival' – God's arrival into the world, born as a baby in Bethlehem. It's such a well-worn story I need hardly go into its details, but therein lies a potential problem, for over-familiarity may well breed apathetic contempt, as happened to the wayward Israelites.

As Christians we've the privileged hindsight and understanding that the baby in the manger grew up to fulfil the Saviour's role. It's a right response at this time of year, therefore, to add emphasis to our thanks for His birth, knowing what future potential lay in that bed of straw. But let's not forget that angels broke through the nonchalant shepherds' darkness, declaring their wonderful message to those who hadn't yet heard (Luke 2:11–12).

As God's twenty-first-century messengers, let's give thought to how we can share the good news among our own generation; to those who merely perceive a baby, rather than Saviour and Lord.

Advent Calendar

For digestion: 'She will give birth to a son, and you are to give him the name Jesus, because he will save his people from their sins' (Matt. 1:21).

For reflection: Picture a newborn baby lying in a feeding trough. What is your response?

Consider or discuss

While some of our friends and family will listen to us talk about the Christ-child, others may have chosen to disbelieve or ignore Him, and may not want us hounding them with every conversation.

- Do you know such folk, and if so has it put you off sharing your message?
- Words are only one way of delivering a message – how else might you use this period of heightened awareness of Christ's birth to make known that He was born to save the world from the penalty of sin?

Prayer

'He is patient with you, not wanting anyone to perish, but everyone to come to repentance' (2 Pet. 3:9).

Lord, grant me Your loving patience and perseverance to make known the Saviour, born as a baby, to those who cannot see in the darkness of life without You (name specific people on your heart).

Pray for others

Pray for church leaders who have increased opportunities to share the gospel, owing to the higher attendance of visitors at Advent and Christmas services. Pray that they would speak the truth with Christ's love, grace, courtesy and power and so encourage visitors to return.

4 DEC

Maintaining Advent love

The heart of the gospel message proclaimed throughout Advent is summed up in John 3:16: 'For God so loved the world that he gave his one and only Son, that whoever believes in him shall not perish but have eternal life.'

Scriptural foundations...

Read Revelation 2:1–7

This beautiful opening salutation depicts Jesus walking among His people, encouraging them for their labour, perseverance and uncompromising endorsement of God's Word. But then He reprimands these faithful Ephesian servants for losing their first love (vv.4–5). While their teaching and service gave an appearance of truth, it had lost its intrinsic significance – personal love for Christ with its subsequent love for others.

God is love (1 John 4:8–9) and Jesus, being the exact representation of His being (Heb. 1:3) expressed that love to humankind through His life. When we believe, receive and fully appreciate His gift of forgiveness and eternal life, our natural response is to love Him. Furthermore, He fills us with His Spirit that we may express His love to each other.

...on which we build

The 'arrival' message of Advent erupts with joyful thanksgiving for God's immense love for the world, accompanied by remembrance praise for the day He birthed our Saviour: 'Glory to God in the highest, and on earth peace to men on whom his favour rests' (Luke 2:14). Nevertheless, we watch as a misguided world fills the Advent period with materialism, drunken revelry and physical indulgence, in a poor attempt to reproduce the ethos of Christian love and joy.

Advent is becoming increasingly renown for its hectic, often stressful preparations, so much so that, despite our faith, we could also become so busy preparing for celebrating the truth as to lose its very essence – to 'Love the Lord your God with all your heart ...' and to 'Love your neighbour as yourself' (Matt. 22:37,39). Love relies on more than mere feelings; it's an active choice of the will. So let's seek new ways to uphold the Advent message in a world that increasingly leaves Christ's love out of Christmas.

Advent Calendar

For digestion: 'By this all men will know that you are my disciples, if you love one another' (John 13:35).
For reflection: Imagine the sad scene of a birthday party in full swing without the 'birthday boy'. Now picture your Advent celebrations: how obvious is Jesus' loving presence?

Consider or discuss

The most popular response to my Advent questionnaire admitted that it's often a period of heightened stress in the church, home and workplace.

- How easy is it to maintain a worshipful focus wherein you continue to express your love for Christ amidst a potentially busier schedule and subsequent increased stress?
- In what way might seasonal pressures diminish your expressions of love to your immediate family and wider circle of friends and acquaintances?
- Being aware of these potential pitfalls, how might you try and avoid them and in what ways could you actively express God's love to others this month?
- ... even to people you don't like?

Prayer

Forgive me, Lord, for the times I feel righteous indignation towards a world that's taking Christ out of Christmas while I'm aware of areas in my own Advent lifestyle which have long since lost Your essence of love:

Take my hands, and let them move
At the impulse of Thy love;
Take my feet, and let them be
Swift and beautiful for Thee.

Take my love; my Lord, I pour
At Thy feet its treasure store:
Take myself, and I will be
Ever, only, all for Thee.
Frances Ridley Havergal, 1836–79

Pray for others
Do you know of anyone who refuses to believe that 'God is love', when surrounded by a world filled with violence, destruction, heartache, injustice and pain? Pray for God's love to melt their hardened hearts. Pray also for those whose only experience is rejection, abuse and hatred.

5 DEC

Advent adverts

Television broadcasts have already been advertising potential Christmas gifts for some weeks, cajoling children and tempting adults to buy or ask for the latest 'must have'. With this and yesterday's reflection in mind, what kind of Advent advert are we?

Scriptural foundations...
Read Matthew 5:13–16

When Jesus taught His disciples atop the mountain, He spoke to a culture without any concept of refrigerators, freezers or chemical preservatives. Salt was their only means of maintaining fresh meat and fish beyond their natural 'shelf life'. Furthermore, those listening to Jesus had never heard of 'light pollution'; but they knew the perils of a pitch-black night, and the difference even one tiny oil lamp could make to guide them on their way.

Our world is decaying, not only physically, but morally and spiritually too. Consequently, it needs a preservative to maintain God's message and values within a godless society. Furthermore, the enemy uses the darkness of immorality and rebellion to blind people from God's truth – but just one light, let alone hundreds and thousands, will make a difference to someone.

...on which we build

Profitable companies wouldn't spend the countless thousands of advertising pounds that they do in the run-up to Christmas, if adverts didn't succeed in their aim of inciting more people to buy their products. How powerful, therefore, is our Advent advert?

It's not always easy to find non-believers genuinely interested in learning about the priceless gift of our Advent focus. Nevertheless, it's our responsibility to preserve and radiate the value of the message and its Messenger throughout our preparations. Are our words and lifestyles a suitable enticement to the joy we've found in knowing God's forgiveness, the hope we have for eternal life, the security we know each day from His love and our expression of it to other people?

We all have the means to influence society as we preserve God's values and message in our lives, and in so doing, shed light into its darkness. Sadly, some will still choose the darkness (John 3:19–21) but others, as a result of our witness, will find God for themselves and praise our Father in heaven (Matt. 5:16).

Advent Calendar

For digestion: 'Your attitude should be the same as that of Christ Jesus' (Phil. 2:5).

For reflection: Picture the part of this decaying world in which you live – what kind of salt and light could you bring into that image?

Consider or discuss

1 Corinthians 13:4–7 pinpoints the fundamental qualities of love. Prayerfully consider how each aspect of love is expressed, or otherwise, through your own life and relationships. Keep this list and its implications in mind throughout your busy day:

Love is…

- patient
- kind

Love…
- does not envy
- does not boast
- is not proud
- is not rude
- is not self-seeking
- is not easily angered
- keeps no record of wrongs
- does not delight in evil

Love always…
- rejoices with the truth
- protects
- trusts
- hopes
- perseveres.

Prayer
Help me, Lord, to be patient when I feel frustrated, kind when I feel fed up, generous when I feel selfish, gracious when I feel rude, forgiving when I feel bitter or proud, persevering when I feel like giving up, and joyful when I feel anything but. Amen.

Pray for others
Who do you find difficult to be nice to, let alone love? Pray for those who harass or persecute you; for 'If you love those who love you, what reward will you get? Are not even the tax collectors doing that? And if you greet only your brothers, what are you doing more than others? Do not even pagans do that?' (Matt 5:46–47).

6 DEC

Advent 'coming'

I was in town yesterday, browsing through an abundant array of Christmas cards on display in a secular retailer, but was particularly saddened by the vast proportion with greetings of Christmas 'magic'.

Scriptural foundations...
Read Daniel 7:1–14

End-time prophecy can seem a bit too strange and wonderful for the human mind to imagine or the heart to understand, including winged beasts, horns that see and speak, a throne emanating thunder and lightning, living creatures with eyes in front and behind (Rev. 4:5–6), a seven-headed dragon (Rev. 12:3) and so on. We shall never fully understand God's higher thoughts and ways, but let's not allow prophetic symbols and metaphors to dissuade us from sharing their crucial implication with others. Jesus is coming again, and anyone whose name is not found in His book of life will be thrown into the lake of fire (Rev. 20:15). Whether we call it hell, eternal separation from God or a place of weeping and gnashing of teeth, not being prepared for the second Advent will be devastating.

...on which we build
There was nothing magical about the arrival of Messiah in Bethlehem; in fact the virgin birth was nothing short of miraculous. Neither will there be anything magical about the Lord's second Advent – majestic and marvellous, but not magical.

As we reflect on Advent past and the Advent to come, secular preparations meanwhile prefer a sprinkle of 'fairy-tale enchantment' – the 'cute' cards, the 'forget-all-my-problems' parties and 'feel-good factor' commercialised hype. The perception of Advent, therefore, can tragically become little more than an entertaining illusion – a season in which personal and world problems are veiled from sight by fairy lights and tinsel; the monotony of unfulfilled lives temporarily uplifted by means of physical pleasures and the short-lived satisfaction of materialism.

So let's not lose sight of the hope that we have for our future, the awesome glory of Jesus' return and the unimaginable splendour of our eternal home. Without such hope, we may be tempted to join others seeking temporary titillations. Living with our glorious hope, however, is a powerful, non-verbal, testimony of faith. It affects our perspective on life and relationships, nurturing our inward well-being with its depth of joy and peace.

Advent Calendar

For digestion: 'At that time the sign of the Son of Man will appear in the sky, and all the nations of the earth will mourn. They will see the Son of Man coming on the clouds of the sky, with power and great glory' (Matt. 24:30).

For reflection: Imagine Jesus returning in His majestic splendour. Does the image excite, inspire, frighten or not affect you at all?

Consider or discuss

Jesus never diluted or avoided telling people the complete truth – but He always spoke with perfect love, gracious humility and a heartfelt concern for the person to whom He was speaking.

- To what extent are you genuinely concerned for other people's eternal future?
- Are you willing to pray for God to create opportunities to communicate this aspect of Advent?

Prayer

Lord, I admit I don't always find it easy to talk to others about judgment. Please instil in my heart a renewed concern for their future and a passion to share the truth of Advent 'coming', seasoned with Your perfect love and grace.

Pray for others

O come, Thou Rod of Jesse, free
Thine own from Satan's tyranny;
From depths of hell Thy people save
And give them victory o'er the grave.

Rejoice, rejoice! Immanuel
Shall come to thee, O Israel.
Tr. John N. Neale, 1818–66, altd

7 DEC

Advent Immanuel

'A merry Christmas, uncle! God save you!'
'Bah! Humbug!' …
'Don't be cross uncle!'

'What else can I be, when I live in such a world of fools as this? Merry Christmas! Out upon merry Christmas! What's Christmas time to you but a time for paying bills without money; a time for finding yourself a year older, but not an hour richer; a time for balancing your books and having every item in 'em through a round dozen of months presented dead against you? If you could work my will, every idiot who goes about with "Merry Christmas" on his lips, should be boiled with his own pudding and buried with a stake of holly through his heart. He should!'

'Uncle!'

'Nephew! Keep Christmas in your own way, and let me keep it in mine.'

(Based on an extract from *A Christmas Carol*, by Charles Dickens)

Scriptural foundations...
Read Isaiah 35:1–10

'…The virgin will be with child and will give birth to a son, and will call him Immanuel' (Isa. 7:14).

Immanuel implies more than mere knowledge of God, more than having His presence dwelling in tabernacles or temples, and more even than the thirty-three years of Jesus' tangible ministry in Israel. Indeed, the fulfilment of this prophecy would bring life into a barren world, a beauty of spirit displaying the glory of God's presence with mankind (Isa. 35:1–2).

Furthermore, by the work of the Lord's own salvation (35:4), it reconciled the way for future believers to know 'God with us' and to one day experience the overwhelming joy of knowing Him face to face (v.10; 1 Cor. 13:12). Meanwhile, as we walk along His 'Way of Holiness', the beauty of that message continues to be revealed to those who don't yet know Him.

...on which we build

I wonder how many people respond to our Advent message with a modern-day 'Bah! Humbug!' And 'humbug' it may well appear unless they perceive the reality for themselves. If Advent is filled with fraught nerves and compromise with our cultural 'festival of commerce', then our message of a Saviour and His coming again might well be trashed as irrelevant. If, however, they can see a positive impact on our own lives, then they too may want it for themselves.

We can spout off theory and theology but the real power of Advent arises from living in close relationship with Immanuel – God with us. Indeed, God of creation, God of Advent past, God of today and God of Advent coming, brings His Life and beauty into this otherwise bleak and sin-filled world.

Advent Calendar

For digestion: '"The virgin will be with child and will give birth to a son, and they will call him Immanuel" – which means, "God with us"' (Matt. 1:23).

For reflection: When others look through the window of your life, would they perceive God living with you?

Consider or discuss

'Keep Christmas in your own way, and let me keep it in mine' (Charles Dickens).

- At times I've been ridiculed for my faith to the point of feeling embarrassed by my lack of scientific or QED answers. But then I remind myself that God – whose ways are far higher than my own – is with me. And He's with you too. No matter how well you feel able to respond to limited human thinking, God will reveal His beauty to others as you continue to walk along His highway of holiness (Isa. 35:8).
- A highway is just as its name suggests; it is raised up and therefore stands out for all to see. How obvious is it that you are walking His way?

Prayer

Lord Immanuel, it's pointless trying to communicate the Advent message without Your help. Holy Spirit, living in my heart, please nurture the beauty of Jesus through each area of my life. Amen.

Pray for others

Do you know someone who has been put off the Christian faith as a result of a poor Christian witness? Pray for them now.

Coming Together Week 1

Space to talk

Allow time to talk through any issues, queries or helpful inspiration that each group member may have from the daily 'Consider or discuss' questions.

Further discussion...

- Swap information about the different resources members use to buy presents, decorations, Advent calendars, cards and so on, which in turn provide meaningful funds for people living and working in poverty, for craftsmen and women running businesses in developing countries, for fairer trade, for organisations spreading the gospel and so on.
- In what ways, if any, do we rely too heavily on our church services or leader to relay the message of our Saviour's birth and His coming again as King, when we each have our own part to play?

Space to reflect

If you find it helpful, light a candle to focus your busy thoughts on the light of Jesus, then ask someone to read the following passage of scripture. Spend a few minutes in silence as you consider how God is speaking to you through His living Word today.

Revelation 1:12–18

Space to pray

Pray together:

Jesus came:
Advent God – we praise You for coming to us in the body of the man Jesus;
  for living among us,
  for working with Your hands,
  for learning, for teaching, for laughing, for weeping.
  For touching the untouchables,
  for loving the unlovable,
  for dying that we might live.

Jesus comes:
Advent God – we thank You for coming to us today through the Holy Spirit;
  for living within us,
  for working through us,
  for teaching and guiding us that we may then help others.
  Use our hands, hearts, minds and wills,
  our homes, resources, work and relationships
  all that we are and all that we have that others might also meet You.

Jesus is coming again:
Advent God – we honour You as supreme King of kings;
  we await with anticipation the glorious day of Your coming to us again,
  we thank you for the hope we have for life in Your eternal presence.

Jesus came, Jesus comes and Jesus is coming again – Hallelujah!

Pray for one another:

Ask each member to write down two or three names of unsaved family or friends, then pass each list to another member of the group. Commit to praying for them throughout December, and if you so choose, into the New Year.

Space to worship

Conclude by singing 'Love Came Down At Christmas' (Christina Rossetti, 1830–94).

If you do not have musicians in the group, try singing (or listening) to it with a CD/taped accompaniment.

Notes

1. Patrick Hanks (ed.), *Collins Dictionary of the English Language* (William Collins, Glasgow, 1979).
2. Figure obtained from the website of the US Center for World Mission: www.uscwm.org
3. Patrick Hanks (ed.), *Collins Dictionary of the English Language* op. cit.
4. For further information contact: Tearcraft (fair trade catalogue for Tearfund), tel. 0870 240 4896/www.tearcraft.org
   TLM Trading (mission catalogue for The Leprosy Mission), tel. 0845 166 2253/www.tlmtrading.com.

WEEK TWO

Preparing for Immanuel

8 DEC

Are you prepared?

We're just into the second week of December and yet I've already been asked a number of times 'Are you ready for Christmas?'

As Advent is the time to prepare to meet Jesus, however, perhaps we should be asking 'Are you ready for Immanuel, God with us?'

Scriptural Foundations...
Read Exodus 25:1–22

God commanded Moses to build the tabernacle and all its furnishings in precise accordance with His instructions, to restore His dwelling with humankind (Exod. 25:8). It didn't come close to the intimacy Adam and Eve experienced when they walked with God in Eden, and it was only a shadow of what was to come. Nevertheless, it was the first exciting step whereby God's people might draw closer to His presence.

We live in a time that the patriarchs were promised and looked towards in faith, but never saw themselves – the time of Immanuel; God living with His people. Meanwhile, they lived with and for God to the extent that He'd revealed Himself within their generation, preparing themselves and their future descendants to be ready for His promised arrival. Just because we live with the promise partially fulfilled, however, does not excuse us from making our own preparations.

...on which we build

'Immanuel' has profound implications on every aspect of life. It's not merely one of the names we hear more often at this time of year; it's not just 'God with us' on Christmas Day or Sundays, when we've been good or while serving in church and so on. It's God with us 24/7. Unfortunately, the impact of this awesome reality may be somewhat diminished if we shrug off its implications in the knowledge that we're saved. If we're prepared to make some adjustments, however, we'll reap the joy and benefits of a life that's learned to dovetail more sweetly into His.

Biblical characters, prophecy and, of course, Christ Himself, provide ample guidelines to prepare a life that befits God's holy ways – guidelines we can adhere to with the help and empowering of the transforming Holy Spirit. I admit we can get distracted from preparing for His presence but I trust, this week, that our biblical forefathers will grant us fresh stimulation.

Advent Calendar

For digestion: 'And surely I am with you always, to the very end of the age' (Matt. 28:20).

For reflection: Take a look at your life. Is your awareness of God's presence verging on continuous or slotted into 'appointment times'; periods of prayer, praise, ministry or teaching, for example?

Consider or discuss

- Have you asked for the further anointing of God's Spirit?
- Are you permitting Him increasing jurisdiction to move within and rule over your life?
- Do you seek the Spirit of the Lord for the sole purpose of supernatural manifestations and feel-good factor sensations, or are you preparing to meet with Him through the routines of daily life?

Prayer

I thank You, Lord Immanuel, for the indwelling of Your Holy Spirit, but I pray for an ever-increasing respect of Your presence as You teach me Your holy ways.

Pray for others

Reflect prayerfully on Paul's words:

'In him the whole building is joined together and rises to become a holy temple in the Lord. And in him you too are being built together to become a dwelling in which God lives by his Spirit' (Eph. 2:21–22).

Pray for Immanuel to express Himself in your local church, through –

Love
Humility
Unity
Grace …

Pray for open doors between local churches, unlocked by –

Love
Humility
Unity
Grace …

Pray for the increasing dwelling of Immanuel through the Church at large, built with –

Love
Humility
Unity
Grace …

9 DEC

Preparing to be a good friend

Friendship has many levels – close friends, distant friends, old friends and new; perhaps you're preparing to meet up with some of them during Advent. But let's also consider preparing to be God's friend, just as Abraham was.

Scriptural foundations …

Read James 2:14–24

God asked Abram to leave his country and people, 'So Abram left, as the LORD had told him …' (Gen. 12:4). God said that despite his old age and lack of children, his heirs would yet become as numerous as the stars: 'Abram believed the LORD, and he credited it to him as righteousness' (Gen. 15:6). Furthermore, when his firstborn, Isaac, was growing up (the first sign of God's promise being fulfilled), God told him to sacrifice the boy on Mount Moriah, and in so doing relinquish the promise that Abraham readily believed: 'Then he reached out his hand and took the knife to slay his son' (Gen. 22:10).

God found a devoted, trusting, obedient friend in Abraham and so He promised to use his offspring as a means to bless all nations (12:3; 22:18). Indeed, the genealogy of Jesus traces right back to him through forty-two generations (Matt. 1:1–17).

...on which we build

Friendships evolve as two people commit to looking out for one another's best interests. But when only one friend puts any effort into the relationship it's unlikely it will deepen and probably won't even last. Many people believe that baby Jesus was born in Bethlehem and so prepare to celebrate 25 December, singing heartily of Immanuel in traditional Christmas carols. Accepting God's presence and friendship, however, demands more than mere belief. For belief to grow into meaningful faith it must be escorted by deeds (James 2:17).

At his inauguration as Archbishop of York in November 2005, Dr John Sentamu said: 'The scandal of the church is that the Christ-event is no longer life-changing, it has become life-enhancing. We've lost the power and joy that makes real disciples, and we've become consumers of religion and not disciples of Jesus Christ.'[1] Indeed, Jesus still seeks out devoted, trustworthy friends – could we be one of them?

Rather than devouring the benefits of belief, let's prepare for dedicated service; and rather than just relying on a comforting 'life-insurance', let's prepare our lives for their exciting role in God's kingdom purposes.

Advent Calendar

For digestion: 'As the body without the spirit is dead, so faith without deeds is dead' (James 2:26).

For reflection: Picture an aged man, pulling together his personal belongings and moving away to an unknown place; standing alone in the darkness and staring up into a star-filled sky; tears streaming down his cheeks with a knife held over his son. How does your devotion compare?

Consider or discuss

- In what ways do you know God as a friend?
- In what ways are you a friend to Him?
- Has God been prompting you to do something which you've resisted because you lack confidence, time or perceived resources?
- Have you given up waiting for a promise God gave you and sought its fulfilment elsewhere?
- Write down your answers and keep yourself accountable before God as you choose to put faith into action.

Prayer

Lord, Immanuel, I am conscious of Your presence with me, urging my faith into meaningful action.

When I'm lazy, stir up zeal;
When I'm unsure, grant me Your vision;
When I'm disobedient, Holy Spirit convict me.
When I feel discouraged, remind me You are there.

Pray for others

Sometimes we can be the answer to our own prayers for other people.

For whom would you like to pray that God would bless or provide for in some way? Regardless whether you know them personally, or whether they live nearby or far away, ask the Lord if you are a part of His answer to your prayer, and if so put your prayer of faith into action.

10 DEC

Preparing for passion

Throughout Advent, children (and some adults) often tell each other what they most want to receive on Christmas Day. David, however, loved nothing and no one more than God – it was his greatest desire to seek God's face all the days of his life (Psa. 27:4); it was this wealthy, handsome, successful king of Israel who yet declared he had nothing good aside from knowing His Lord (Psa. 16:2); and it was David who danced before God with all his might regardless of being ridiculed (2 Sam. 6:14–22).

Scriptural foundations...

Read Psalm 23

David's psalms portray the divine Character he'd grown to know and love passionately – a provider (65:9), a refuge and strong tower in times of trouble (61:3), a helper and protective shadow (63:7), a Saviour and burden bearer (68:19); One who answers the heartfelt cry (40:1) with unfailing love and abundant compassion (51:1).

Other kings believed in God but trusted more in the wisdom and strength of men. Conversely, David *knew* God and therefore put his trust in Him alone; and it was David who played his part in God's ongoing promise to Abraham (2 Sam. 7:16). Twenty-eight generations later, Mary gave birth to our Saviour who would reign on David's throne forever (Luke 1:31–33).

...on which we build

Occasionally my husband has been chatting to someone after a Sunday service when, unbeknown to him, a toddler draws alongside, mistaking him for their own dad. The surprise of feeling a tiny hand reaching up to clasp his has profound effect – this sense of implicit loving trust. Such faith is touching in the right situation, but results in tragic consequences when placed into the wrong hands.

Immanuel – God is with you and with me. Whether we're as passionate for His presence as David was and as willing to keep our hand in His, may depend on how well we know Him, how much we appreciate what He's done for us and to what degree we rely on Him for our lives. As wary adults we're not as trusting as youngsters, but our passion for God will grow as we experience His unfailing love through a deepening, personal relationship; and no one else can do it on our behalf.

Advent Calendar

For digestion: '… who is he who will devote himself to be close to me?' (Jer. 30:21)
For reflection: Picture God looking into your heart then writing down a list of the five things, relationships and/or activities that He sees are most important to you. Who or what would He write down first?

Consider or discuss

'You will seek me and find me when you seek me with all your heart' (Jer. 29:13).

- What or who do you seek half- or wholeheartedly: Immanuel, worldly success, personal comforts, independence, tradition, human relationships and so on?
- Who or what would you struggle to live without?
- Do you rely on *feelings* to express your love for God, or do you *choose* to love Him with your prayers, words, actions and lifestyle?

Prayer

If only I possessed the grace, good Jesus,
to be utterly at one with you!
Amidst all the variety of world things around me,
Lord, the only thing I crave is you.
You are all my soul needs.
Unite, dear friend of my heart,
this unique little soul of mine to your perfect goodness.
You are all mine;
when shall I be yours?
Lord Jesus, my beloved,
be the magnet of my heart;
clasp, press, unite me for ever to your sacred heart.
You have made me for yourself;

make me one with you.
Absorb this tiny drop of life
into the ocean of goodness from whence it came.
Prayer of St Francis de Sales, 1567–1622

Pray for others

Pray for renewed passion for Jesus throughout the Christian community.

11 DEC

Preparing to seek God's heart

Depending on whom we're obliged to visit during this period and whether we've teenagers making demands at home, Advent may include a juggling act of people-pleasing. As we prepare for Immanuel, however, it's His heart primarily we should now be seeking to please.

Scriptural foundations...

Read Acts 13:21–38

When Saul was stripped of his crown and kingdom, God chose a successor who was prepared to submit unreservedly to His will. Indeed, David was described as a man after God's own heart (1 Sam. 13:14) – zealous to know His will, ways and purpose. That's why God trusted him as king, knowing he would obey whatever was asked of him (Acts 13:22). And so he continued to serve and complete God's purpose within his own generation (Acts 13:36).

He was anointed as Israel's king; he was a champion warrior, successful in purging Israel's enemies from the land; he accumulated wealth in preparation for God's Temple; he used his skills as a musician and poet to minister to others; he trained up his son to succeed him, and was a 'shepherd of God's flock', relating to and having compassion for God's people.

David fulfilled his purpose which not only impacted his own

generation but continues to encourage and teach us, almost 3,000 years later.

...on which we build

Paul reminds us to do everything without complaining or arguing, 'for it is God who works in you to will and to act according to his good purpose' (Phil. 2:13–14). But isn't it easier to do things for someone whom you love? I don't think twice about keeping house for my family, but I might well have to think ten times before doing it for someone I didn't even like!

It's in getting to know God that we love Him, and the more we love Him the more we long to know His heart – His will for our lives, His purpose in our part of the world. Jesus only did what He saw His Father doing (John 5:19), and so as Immanuel walks with us, we too can seek our Father's heart then simply get right on with it. After all, He didn't mould our unique role to fit anyone else at any other time; rather, it was especially designed for you and for me to be fulfilled in this generation (Eph. 2:10).

Advent Calendar

For digestion: 'I consider my life worth nothing to me, if only I may finish the race and complete the task the Lord Jesus has given me …' (Acts 20:24).
For reflection: Take another look behind the door of your heart. Whose dreams and purposes can you see vying for your attention?

Consider or discuss

- How often do you spend time listening in prayer to God's ongoing purposes?
- Do you recognise different 'seasons' in your life as God moves you from one task to another? If so, can you recognise God's hand of preparation on your life to bring you to the place you are today?

Prayer

Eternal God,
the light of the minds that know you,
the joys of the hearts that love you,

and the strength of the wills that serve you;
grant us so to know you, that we may truly love you,
and so to love you, that we may fully serve you,
whom to serve is perfect freedom,
in Jesus Christ our LORD.
Gelasian Sacramentary[2]

Pray for others
Pray 'for kings and all those in authority, that we may live peaceful and quiet lives in all godliness and holiness. This is good, and pleases God our Saviour' (1 Tim. 2:2–3).

12 DEC

Preparing with thanksgiving

'If you take Christ out of Christmas, all you're left with is M & S'[3]! Paul Wilson's light-hearted jibe at Christmas commerce makes me smile, yet it stirs up serious undertones, for Advent preparations are meaningless devoid of the cross of Christ. Without it, our remembrance of His birth would be pointless and our anticipation of His return, futile.

Scriptural foundations...
Read 1 Corinthians 1:18–31

Just under 400 years after David was laid to rest with his ancestors, Jeremiah prophesied, '... I will raise up to David a righteous Branch, a King who will reign wisely and do what is just and right in the land. ... This is the name by which he will be called: The LORD Our Righteousness' (Jer. 23:5–6).

God, being perfectly holy, cannot look upon sin (Hab. 1:13), to do so would cause the immediate death of that upon which He looked (Rom. 6:23). In order to live with His people, however, He permitted a system of animal sacrifice whose shed blood covered their unrighteousness. But through Abraham's seed and David's heir, God promised the world a Kingly Saviour who would do away with that monotonous system. Indeed, the Lord would become our 'righteousness, holiness and redemption' (1 Cor. 1:30).

...on which we build

'Xmas' has been familiar shorthand for some years, but more recent political correctness in the guise of 'anti-religious hatred' is trying to take Christ's name out of our Christmas celebrations, 'For the message of the cross is foolishness to those who are perishing …' Nevertheless, God with us by His Holy Spirit results from Christ's righteous blood covering over our sin, so '… to us who are being saved it is the power of God' (1 Cor. 1:18).

If you're experiencing frazzled nerves or simply feeling down owing to the busy Christmas lead-up, take a moment to pause and remember the reason for your frantic preparations. Jesus suffered indescribable pain that we might know 'Immanuel' in our twenty-first-century celebrations. Take time to say thank you once again for what Jesus did for you.

Advent Calendar

For digestion: 'For it is by grace you have been saved, through faith – and this not from yourselves, it is the gift of God – not by works, so that no-one can boast' (Eph. 2:8–9).

For reflection: Picture a large, white-bearded man clad in red coat, fur-trimmed hat and black boots! Children are told they must be good if Santa's to leave them any presents – but we cannot earn the priceless presence of God; it's an undeserved gift, an act of grace.

Consider or discuss

Reflect on the range of circumstances Jesus endured in order that we may know Immanuel – God with us – today

- Having left the perfection, holiness and splendour of heaven, He was born as a human into poverty, became a refugee, and then lived under occupying forces.
- He experienced hunger, grief, hardship and temptation alongside other difficulties.
- In the latter years of His life, He was homeless and without a financial income.

- He was betrayed by one of His closest friends.
- He was verbally abused and horrifically tortured.
- But perhaps His greatest suffering arose from being separated from His Father as He took on all our sin at the point of His death.

Prayer

Immanuel, O Immanuel,
Bowed in awe I worship at Your feet,
And sing Immanuel, God is with us;
Sharing my humanness, my shame,
Feeling my weaknesses, my pain,
Taking the punishment, the blame,
Immanuel.
And now my words cannot explain,
All that my heart cannot contain,
How great are the glories of Your name,
Immanuel.
Graham Kendrick[4]

Pray for others

Pray for any political leaders in the world who perceive the cross to be foolish and attempt to ban its message of God's perfect love and forgiveness.

13 DEC

Preparing God's home

I wonder what similarities or differences we have in preparing our church or home during Advent. Some of us may have an Advent wreath, candles and purple cloths, or we may prefer the modern use of tinsel, trees and trinkets. No matter how we prepare our home for an event or special guests, we are reminded of our greater need to prepare a home for Immanuel.

Scriptural foundations...
Read Joel 2:28–32

Throughout the Old Testament and the beginning of the New, God chose to anoint certain individuals with His Spirit in order to fulfil specific tasks; Bezalel (Exod. 31:3), Gideon (Judg. 6:34), David (1 Sam. 16:13), John the Baptist (Luke 1:15–17) and Mary (Luke 1:35), for example. Nevertheless, Joel prophesied of a day when God's Spirit would pour out upon everyone; and not just for a specific purpose, but for deeper knowledge and relationship with God.

A few 'nativity' characters visited and worshipped the newborn Saviour. Yet, it wasn't until He became a man that twelve disciples began to grasp the concept of Almighty God living with humble mankind. In fact, they became accustomed to Jesus being with them; teaching, advising, comforting, disciplining, providing, praying, nurturing and so on. It was a rude shock, despite His warnings, when they lost Him to the cross but, just a few weeks later, His Spirit came to live with them permanently (John 14:17).

...on which we build
'... If anyone loves me, he will obey my teaching. My Father will love him, and we will come to him and make our home with him' (John 14:23).

The disciples gained an intimacy with Jesus surpassing anything they'd known previously. After the outpouring of the Spirit at Pentecost, His teaching, guidance, comfort and counsel emanated from a 24/7 Immanuel – God living deep within, making a home in their hearts.

Most of us have our own ideas of what constitutes 'home', and decorate, renovate, clean or furnish it accordingly. Likewise, when God is given the keys to our lives His Spirit comes to live within, but He'll then ask us to work with Him to bring about some changes – renovations to His home that befit His holy presence. Indeed, it's the power of His Spirit that transforms us, but we've still got to choose to align our ways to His.

Advent Calendar
For digestion: 'Do you not know that your body is a temple of the

Holy Spirit, who is in you, whom you have received from God? You are not your own; you were bought at a price. Therefore honour God with your body' (1 Cor. 6:19–20).

For reflection: Picture a young girl called Mary, the first human tabernacle, the dwelling place of Jesus – Immanuel. Now you are the home for God's Spirit.

Consider or discuss

'Greetings, you who are highly favoured! The Lord is with you' (Luke 1:28).

- The Lord is with you too. What changes might you make to honour His presence and make Him feel more at home in your life?
- Are there any 'rooms' that you'd prefer He didn't enter?

Prayer

Lord, the house of my soul is narrow:
Enlarge it, that you may enter in.
It is ruined:
O repair it!
It displeases you:
I confess it, I know.
But who shall cleanse it,
to whom shall I cry but to you?
Lord, cleanse me from secret faults
and spare your servant from strange sins.

Prayer of St Augustine of Hippo, 354–430

Pray for others

'… I am again in the pains of childbirth until Christ is formed in you' (Gal. 4:19). Seek Paul's passion for other people as you pray for those who want to know about God but who are not willing to know Immanuel in relationship through the Spirit.

14 DEC

Ongoing preparations

My favourite time of the Advent and Christmas period is the evening of Christmas Eve. It's too late to buy any more gifts, prepare any more food, send any more cards, put up any more tinsel or practise any more carols. At last I can sit and savour the results of those weeks of preparations, congratulating myself on a job well done while anticipating the fruit of all that hard labour!

Preparing for Immanuel, however, continues until the day He comes again. There's no such thing as an annual 'Christmas Eve' to complete our preparations – we'll be fine-tuning our lives until the day we meet Him in eternity.

Scriptural foundations...
Read Ephesians 3:14–21

Moses is the only man since the Fall to have spoken with God face to face (Exod. 33:11), for he 'was a very humble man, more humble than anyone else on the face of the earth' (Num. 12:3). The radiant physical effects of living so intimately with God caused him to wear a veil when mingling with the people (Exod. 34:33–35).

We won't see God's face until we leave this world to be with Him in eternity, but we can seek an ever-increasing infilling of His Spirit. We are sealed with the Holy Spirit upon our first confession of faith (Eph. 1:13), but let's also prepare more room in our lives to be 'filled to the measure of all the fullness of God' (Eph. 3:19). In doing so it will resource our human limitations with divine power while increasing the measure of God that other people perceive.

...on which we build
With Christmas eleven days away, I've had to make space in my home for extra guests and for all those gifts I might receive! I've sorted out the cupboards of unused belongings for charity, I've sent my empty cardboard boxes to the rubbish tip, and when my daughter was younger, I used to clear out her playthings of broken toys or outgrown games to make way for the new. Similarly, the

more space we prepare for Jesus, the more He'll fill our lives. It's a simple equation but one that might get overlooked by other Advent preparations.

I've also been cleaning and tidying up the house. It's a never-ending job – and so too with the home we provide for Immanuel. A dirty house may make me feel uncomfortable, but apathy concerning unconfessed sin, grieves the Spirit intensely. He washes us completely on our first confession of faith, but our imperfect lives can't help being scuffed by our fallen world and nature (John 13:10). So let's use this reminder to clear out the debris of self, confess our sin, and thereby maintain a suitable home for our holy Immanuel.

Advent Calendar

For digestion: 'And we, who with unveiled faces all reflect the Lord's glory, are being transformed into his likeness with ever-increasing glory, which comes from the Lord, who is the Spirit' (2 Cor. 3:18).
For reflection: Seeing your life as a home for Immanuel, how scuffed and stained is it looking, and what is filling each room?

Consider or discuss

Consider once again, your ongoing Advent preparations:

- What dominates them: preparing your heart for Immanuel or preparing decorations, presents, cards, food and so on?
- Can the two be linked?
- Jesus didn't just come to be part of a wonderful story – He came to impact our lives. Are you content with being 'sealed' with the Spirit, or do you truly hunger to be filled 'to the measure'?

Prayer

Open wide the window of our spirits and fill us full of light;
Open wide the door of our hearts, that we may receive and entertain Thee with all our powers of adoration and love.
Christina Rossetti, 1830–94

Pray for others

Who is on your heart for prayer?

Adapt today's reading to pray for them – as named individuals or groups.

Coming Together Week 2

Space to talk

Allow time to talk through any issues, queries or helpful inspiration that each group member may have from the daily 'Consider or discuss' questions.

Further discussion...

- Re-read the extract from Archbishop Dr John Sentamu's inauguration speech (see 9 December: '... on which we build') and discuss your response.
- Consider the different implication between getting to *know* God better (Eph. 1:17) compared with our inability to fully *understand* God's higher thoughts and ways (Isa. 55:8–9).
- Share with each other the potential impact of maintaining a home in your lives – a temple – for God's Holy Spirit.

Space to reflect

If you find it helpful, light a candle to focus your busy thoughts on the light of Jesus, then ask someone to read the following passage of Scripture. Spend a few minutes in silence as you consider how God is speaking to you through His living Word today.

Acts 2:1–21

Space to pray

Pray together:

Immanuel, God with us – we long to experience Your presence.

Immanuel whose purpose prevails – dovetail our desires with Yours.

Immanuel whose dwelling is with us – make Your home in our hearts.

Amen.

Pray for one another:
Split into pairs and share one or more of the areas that you want to be accountable for (see 9 December 'Consider or discuss') then pray for each other.

Space to worship
Conclude by singing 'From Heaven You Came' (Graham Kendrick, 1983 Kingsway's Thankyou Music).

If you do not have musicians in the group, try singing (or listening) to it with a CD/taped accompaniment.

Notes

1. www.cofe.anglican.org/news
2. *Gathering for Worship*, The Baptist Union of Great Britain (Canterbury Press, Norwich, 2005).
3. J. John and Mark Stibbe, *A Box of Delights* (Monarch, London, 2001) p.29.
4. Graham Kendrick © 1988 Make Way Music. www.grahamkendrick.co.uk Used with permission.

WEEK THREE

Immanuel: For Better, for Worse

15 DEC

Immanuel: In the fiery furnace

Despite the famous line, 'Joy to the world', Advent for many folk is wracked by heartache and pain: '…this time of year can bring more than its fair share of stress, noise, anxiety and squabbles. Add this to long-standing money worries, family conflicts, job problems or bereavement, and it's no wonder calls to helplines about depression and suicide rise by nearly ten per cent during the festive season' (Dr Trisha Macnair).[1]

Scriptural foundations…
Read Daniel 3:13–30

The story of Shadrach, Meshach and Abednego, speaks for itself; pressurised to bow down to idols, but refusing to compromise. The heat was on – literally! With the reality of death's fiery flames staring them in the face they held fast to their dependence on the God whom they professed. In fact, they not only reiterated their faith that God had the power to save them, but expressed implicit trust in His loving faithfulness, regardless of the outcome of their difficult situation.

These men broke the boundaries of 'eleventh hour' problem-solving, moving into a realm where only God could relieve their plight. And that's exactly where they found His presence – walking right beside them in the centre of the furnace.

...on which we build

The angels brought 'good news of great joy ... for all the people' (Luke 2:10). But not every Christian would testify to experiencing great joy during this season of Advent. In fact, the lonely, the poor, the bereaved, the rejected, the sick, the jobless, the persecuted and so on, may well find Advent the most difficult time of the year.

Believing the gospel message of love, forgiveness and eternal life is the most fantastic news we could ever hear, but doesn't stop us feeling the repercussions of living in a fallen world, grappling with imperfect relationships. So, let's read once again the angel's message for, as Al Mawhinney writes, 'No one's life situation is so terrifying that they aren't included in "all the people". No one's desperation is so great that it scares Jesus away. The Christmas story is that Jesus came "for all the people."'[2]

If the experience of joy seems far beyond our reach, let's dare to open our eyes and look for Immanuel – God with us in the fiery heat of adversity; and may our Advent focus enrich our heart's response.

Advent Calendar

For digestion: '"Never will I leave you; never will I forsake you." So we say with confidence, "The Lord is my helper; I will not be afraid. What can man do to me?"' (Heb. 13:5–6)

For reflection: Picture yourself facing your difficulty then place yourself within the protective shadow of Almighty God.

Consider or discuss

Consider a massive furnace turned up to full heat, in the centre of which someone is walking with God.

- Who is that person?
- What do the flames symbolise?
- Can they perceive God with them or do they need reassurance that He's there?

Prayer

Forgive me, Lord, if I've ever dismissed hurting people from my conscience with a pious platitude of prayer. Thank You that I do not have to carry their burden but may the compassion and comfort that You've shown to me overflow to those I know experiencing heartache and trouble.

Pray for others

In 2004, the United Kingdom granted an average 457 divorces per day;[3] 140,000 people attempt suicide each year in England and Wales;[4] twenty-four million items of anti-depressant drugs were dispensed in England in 2001;[5] and more than 100,000 families in England and Wales live in temporary accommodation (including an estimated 150,000 children) with a further 400,000 'non-statutory' people living in hostels, squats, on friends' floors and in overcrowded accommodation.[6]

'Immanuel, You came with good news for *all* people. Oh Lord, teach us to pray ...'

16 DEC

Immanuel: Indwelling our loneliness

'A call every seven seconds is expected by Samaritans this Christmas and New Year ... "Seeing everyone else apparently having fun all around them can be really tough, especially if they are on their own, or even if they are with family and friends."'[7] Indeed, for some who completed my Advent questionnaire, it's the worst time of year to feel intensified loneliness.

Scriptural foundations...

Read 2 Timothy 4:9–18

Alone in a cold, dark, dank, rank Roman prison, Paul's plea for his friends and his beloved 'son' Timothy (1 Cor. 4:17) is heart-wrenching. This tremendous man of faith, self-sacrifice, love, compassion and zeal, felt desperately lonely. Furthermore, at his preliminary hearing before the Roman court he'd been completely alone, deserted perhaps by those who feared for their own lives or who simply couldn't get there in time.

Paul reached out for the comforting companionship of close friends but, meanwhile clung to the knowledge of His Lord, whose presence provided uncompromising strength of faith in the face of persecution. Indeed, these were Paul's last words to Timothy, the Early Church and to us today; profound teaching laced with human vulnerability.

...on which we build

Loneliness has many guises – it can manifest when physically alone, but also prevails in a crowd; it arises from memories of loved ones, but also from longed-for relationships that never came into being; it may result from rejection, but just as much from feeling that you simply don't 'fit in'.

Like Paul, we may all seek 'God with us' in a unique personal relationship; to know that we are never alone for His Spirit is always with us (John 16:7; Matt. 28:20). As we trust Him, despite feeling vulnerable, to help us face our pain, we may then find Immanuel – God with us in the heart of our loneliness.

Nevertheless, 'God sets the lonely in families …' (Psa 68:6). It's therefore our prerogative as the family of Christ to be a part of God's answer to loneliness so that '… no-one misses the grace of God …' (Heb. 12:15). So, let's 'Share with God's people who are in need. Practise hospitality … be sympathetic, love as brothers, be compassionate and humble' (Rom. 12:13; 1 Pet. 3:8). Such are the Advent preparations we might all be involved with to express God's love to the lonely.

Advent Calendar

For digestion: 'Look to my right and see; no-one is concerned for me. I have no refuge; no-one cares for my life. I cry to you, O LORD; I say, "You are my refuge, my portion in the land of the living"' (Psa. 142:4–5).

For reflection: Picture the faces of people in your church, neighbourhood, workplace and community. Whose loneliness does God see that might otherwise go unnoticed?

Consider or discuss

'... My God, my God, why have you forsaken me?' (Matt. 27:46).

- Immanuel empathises with loneliness; He experienced it in the wilderness and in His itinerant ministry; when He was misunderstood, deserted by His closest friends, rejected by the once loving crowds, and abandoned by His Father on the cross.
- How can you help to fill the void of other people's loneliness – during Advent, Christmas, New Year and beyond?

Prayer

'I am with you all the days (perpetually, uniformly, and on every occasion)...' (Matt. 28:20b, Amplified)

Immanuel – God is with me.

Although I feel lonely,
You are with me;
  Perpetually: permanently, constantly, twenty-four hours of each and every day.
You are with me;
  Uniformly: unchangingly, unfailingly, my steadfast unshakeable security.
You are with me;
  On every occasion: no matter where I am, no matter who I'm with, no matter what I'm doing.

Holy Spirit, please embed this truth into the depths of my lonely heart.
  Amen.

Pray for others

Pray for short- or long-term missionaries abroad who may feel increasingly homesick at this time of year. If you know any personally, how might God use you to answer that prayer with practical love and encouragement?

17 DEC

Immanuel: Binding up broken hearts

Irving Berlin's 'White Christmas', bids for a high position amongst the most popular secular seasonal songs, owing perhaps to nostalgic yearnings for memories of Christmas past – 'Just like the ones I used to know'. But nostalgia ignores the wracking ache of bereavement, the gut-wrenching insecurity of job loss, the ultimate rejection served up in final divorce papers and so on.

Scriptural foundations...
Read Isaiah 61:1–3

Isaiah's vision of Messiah, the Anointed One, promised comfort, hope, transformation and vengeance; and it was to this very passage of Scripture that Jesus turned in His hometown Nazareth synagogue. Nevertheless, He only referred to the first one and a half verses (Luke 4:16–19), indicating the rest would be fulfilled at His second coming.

'Broken-hearted' infers shattered emotions, spirit or mind. How wonderful, therefore, that the original Hebraic translation implies 'a personal ministry of soothing and healing ... any and every human breakdown'.[8] If we've been walking through a fiery furnace and can only see a heap of ash where once was life and purpose, Immanuel brings good news, both now and for the future.

...on which we build
Whether or not our heart broke during Advent, on Christmas Day or during the preceding year(s), December festivities heighten the senses to the intensity of our loss. Consequently, Advent preparations for a Christmas filled with tears can be unbearable.

Jesus may sound ironic when we first hear Him say, 'Blessed are those who mourn, for they will be comforted' (Matt. 5:4), for how can feeling sad become the means to finding happiness? The sentiment may apply to grief over personal sin but in the context of mourning personal loss, Eugene Peterson provides a most helpful translation: 'You're blessed when you feel you've lost what is most dear to you. Only then can you be embraced by the One most dear to you' (Matt. 5:4, *The Message*).

Our Wonderful Counsellor weeps with us, but longs to fill that aching hole our sorrowful loss has left. Whatever the cause of a broken heart, Immanuel resides deep within to help us let go of its shattered components, in order for Him to bind it back together.

Advent Calendar

For digestion: 'Jesus wept' (John 11:35).
For reflection: Picture a pile of ashes and a broken heart. Invite Jesus into this image and trust Him to make them into something new and beautiful.

Consider or discuss

Jesus was the Son of God but remained fully human, experiencing the sorrows of this world as much as the joys of His message.

- Immanuel appreciates the need for time to grieve alone (Matt. 14:13).
- Immanuel experienced a troubled spirit (John 11:33–35).
- Immanuel's sorrow shed burning tears (Luke 19:41–42).
- To whom can you offer Immanuel's physical embrace and soothing touch?

Prayer

Lord, I long for the day when there shall be
    no more tears,
    no more sadness,
    no more pain.
Meanwhile, Immanuel – God with me at this, and every moment,
  sustain me,
  uphold me,
  protect me,
and bind up completely my aching, broken heart.

Pray for others

Call to mind any people you know who've been broken by life's troubles…

Lord, You are close to the broken-hearted and save those who are crushed in spirit (Psa. 34:18). Bring to them the comfort of Your embrace, the security of Your unfailing love, the light of Your presence to guide them into the future.

Lord, You've anointed me with Your Spirit, too, help me to share Your good news in a meaningful, tangible way. Amen.

18 DEC

Immanuel: Veiled by the darkness of despair

'... we who are Christians need always to be sensitive to one another's circumstances and problems *but never so much as at Christmas*' (Selwyn Hughes).[9]

Scriptural foundations...
Read Psalm 77

Distressed, sleepless, inconsolable and dispirited – in short, depressed and despairing. Such was the psalmist's honest lament. The absence of feeling God's presence and power filled his vulnerable heart with doubt; doubting God's acceptance, blessing, love, faithfulness, mercy and compassion.

It's not unusual to feel overwhelmed by difficulty, nor even to question where God has gone when sorrow, confusion, disappointment, and so on, smother our tangible senses with bleakest despair. And perhaps it feels more pertinent in this season of Advent joy. So what is the answer when we cannot *feel* Immanuel, God with us? 'Then ...' the psalmist counsels, we need to remember and consider His deeds, meditate on His works, and declare His holy ways (vv.10–13).

It's not acting on feeling but acting in faith. It won't eject us out of our pit but will give us strength for the climb. It may not immediately put a smile on our face but steadfastly build up our heart – scattering doubt and uncertainty in the light of unfailing love. It will give praise where praise is due, despite our present troubles.

...on which we build

Isaiah's prophetic answer to Israel's plight speaks of the Lord's anointed Servant, 'He will not shout or cry out, or raise his voice in the streets. A bruised reed he will not break, and a smouldering wick he will not snuff out ...' (Isa. 42:2–3). Empowered by the Spirit yet infinitely gentle, Immanuel inspires hope in His capabilities while endearing our trust through His tender touch. This is God with you and with me in the darkness of despair. Perhaps we cannot see or feel Him, but He will not shout or give us a good shake and tell us it's high time we sorted ourselves out. Rather, He climbs into our pit of despair to be with us and to encourage our climb back out – in His strength, in His way and in His perfect time.

To trust God in the bleakest of circumstances we need to get to know Him – to comprehend the unfailing nature of the One who has promised to stay with us. So let's choose to build up our faith for the climb by remembering and declaring His loving faithfulness.

Advent Calendar

For digestion: '... Though I have fallen, I will rise. Though I sit in darkness, the LORD will be my light' (Micah 7:8).

For reflection: Imagine a lone figure slumped on the floor of a deep, dark chasm, lacking any hope for their future. Bring to mind some images of what God has done in the past and draw them into your picture.

Consider or discuss

- Are you prepared to reach out in faith for Immanuel – even if you can't see Him in the darkness?
- Will you hold on to Him and trust Him to take care of you?
- How sensitive are your words and behaviour with people who currently lack hope for their future?

Prayer

I'm struggling for air, Lord,
it's so dark I can't even see.
I'm shivering but I'm not cold,
I ache inside though I'm not unwell.

I can't hear You, Lord,
where are You?...

I believe in You, Almighty God, Creator of the universe,
leaving Your heavenly glory to be with me.
I will trust You, Immanuel;
I will hold on to Your eternal love,
unfailing compassion,
Sovereign purpose,
and tender touch.
You will be the light in my darkness,
the healer of my soul,
the voice to break my silence,
the constant companion at my side.

'I do believe; help me overcome my unbelief!' (Mark 9:24)
Amen.

Pray for others

Pray specifically for someone you know suffering with despair:

Immanuel, shine Your light into their darkness;
Spirit within them, strengthen their weakened frame.
Immanuel, breathe life into their soul,
Lord at their side, meet with their desperation.

19 DEC

Immanuel: Facing our fear

One of the messages we repeatedly hear in nativity plays and carol services is the timeless call of the angels: 'Do not be afraid ...' – Zechariah, Mary, Joseph, shepherds. But for many of us, it's easier to say than to actually put into practice.

Scriptural foundations...

Read Psalm 46

Fleeing from their Egyptian captors the Israelites encountered a dead end and were terrified (Exod. 14:10). But Moses countered their frantic cries, saying 'The LORD will fight for you; you need only to be still' (Exod. 14:14). Years later, when David trembled before his enemies he too learnt this lesson: 'Be still before the LORD and wait patiently for him; do not fret when men succeed in their ways …' (Psa. 37:7).

And although catastrophe surrounded the psalmist in today's reading, he focused on the fact that the Lord Almighty was with him, a permanent refuge and support (Psa. 46:7). In so doing, he received and recorded the divine response for generations to come: 'Be still, and know that I am God …' (v.10). Still your heart, mind, body and soul; recognise who I am and let Me walk with you and talk with you throughout this difficult time.

...on which we build

What fears preoccupy your thoughts and feelings as you prepare for Christmas and look beyond to the New Year? Who or what causes you to feel anxious, distressed, apprehensive or alarmed?

Fear is a feeling whereas God with us is fact. Fear may give rise to all manner of physical and psychological symptoms, but knowing God with us gives rise to an inexplicable depth of peace and calm, far surpassing our limited understanding (Phil. 4:7).

God keeps reminding us not to let fear overwhelm us, but to do so we'll need to develop the art of being still – stilling our frantic thoughts, stopping ourselves from racing here and there, and sitting still with Immanuel. It grants space and time for the Spirit to do His work, reminding us Who is in control, Who is all-knowing, all-loving all-powerful; and Who is with us every minute of each day.

Be still, and know Immanuel.

Advent Calendar

For digestion: 'I am the LORD, your God, who takes hold of your right hand and says to you, Do not fear; I will help you' (Isa. 41:13).
For reflection: Picture yourself sitting among the people or

situations that cause you to feel afraid. What are you focusing on – everything around you or God who presides over your life?

Consider or discuss

- Are you afraid of someone? Meditate on Hebrews 13:6.
- Are you afraid of death? Meditate on Hebrews 2:14–15.
- Are you afraid of life? Meditate on 2 Timothy 1:7.
- Are you afraid of God? Meditate on 1 John 4:18.
- Are you afraid of financial difficulty? Meditate on Luke 12:29–31.
- Are you afraid of persecution? Meditate on Luke 12:11–12.
- Are you afraid of what people think about you? Meditate on Galatians 1:10.

Prayer

'Listen to my prayer, O God, do not ignore my plea; hear me and answer me. My thoughts trouble me and I am distraught ... My heart is in anguish within me; the terrors of death assail me. Fear and trembling have beset me; horror has overwhelmed me. I said, "Oh, that I had the wings of a dove! I would fly away and be at rest" ... But I call to God, and the LORD saves me. Evening, morning and noon I cry out in distress, and he hears my voice. He ransoms me unharmed from the battle waged against me ... as for me, I trust in you.' Amen.

(From Psalm 55)

Pray for others

Pray for people who are trained or gifted in helping others face their fears, including the Samaritans, counsellors and so on.

20 DEC

Immanuel: Through persecution

Advent preparations focus on the wonder and joy of Christ's coming to bring peace between humanity and God – an awesome occasion to celebrate. The peace we find through restored relationship with

God, however, may conversely incite conflict in relationships with non-believers (Matt. 10:34).

Scriptural foundations...

Read Luke 21:10–19

'... In this world you will have trouble ...' (John 16:33a). Whether or not we've suffered any form of persecution by means of insults, rejection, withdrawal of essential provisions, imprisonment, torture or the threat of death, our only option is to place our trust in Jesus, who went on to say, '... But take heart! I have overcome the world' (v.33b).

It's not easy to 'take heart' when we read scriptural, historical and ongoing reports of Christian persecution but, no matter what we encounter while passing through this world, God will always be with us. Thus the importance of knowing Immanuel in personal relationship by His Spirit, without which we may well lack the necessary courage to spur us on.

So, 'Let us fix our eyes on Jesus, the author and perfecter of our faith, who for the joy set before him endured the cross, scorning its shame, and sat down at the right hand of the throne of God. Consider him who endured such opposition from sinful men, so that you will not grow weary and lose heart' (Heb. 12:2–3).

...on which we build

For many years, the term 'Christian persecution' has been used for the suffering Church overseas but, more recently, numerous reports confirm its growth on our very own doorstep, often disguised in the name of 'political correctness'. Even as I've been writing this book I've read many such reports, including the following: the Havant Borough Council removed the word Christmas from the turning-on ceremony and renamed it the Festival of Lights;[10] the Home Office threatened to stop funding a carol service for the victims of crime because it is 'too Christian';[11] the Inland Revenue prevented staff donating money to their usual charity because of its Christian links;[12] and a Christian couple faced an eighty-minute police interrogation for complaining to the Wyre Borough Council about its promotion of homosexuality.[13]

While we probably wouldn't choose the emotional or physical pain that persecution can invoke, it's part and parcel of our faith. Knowing Immanuel and trusting in His presence, however, we too, like Jesus, can learn to face our 'cross' in whatever form it takes, that we may seek to know His joy and reap our heavenly reward.

Advent Calendar

For digestion: '"Father, if you are willing, take this cup from me; yet not my will, but yours be done." An angel from heaven appeared to him and strengthened him' (Luke 22:42–43).
For reflection: Picture Jesus facing verbal and physical abuse, and yet He maintained strength and dignity. Jesus, living in you, will encourage and enable you likewise.

Consider or discuss

Consider the following scriptures that may encourage you in your own sufferings or help you to stand alongside many who are suffering elsewhere:

- Christ's power is enhanced by the weakness you feel through persecution (2 Cor. 12:9–10).
- Persecution reminds you to lean on God rather than on yourself (2 Cor. 1:8–9).
- Nothing, including persecution, can separate you from the love of Immanuel (Rom. 8:35–39).
- If you do not currently suffer persecution, how do you support those who do (Heb. 13:3)?

Prayer

Almighty God,
 You know how it feels to be rejected, disbelieved, ignored –
And yet You keep loving Your enemies.

Loving Lord Jesus,
 You know how it feels to be misunderstood, ridiculed, tortured –
And yet You forgave Your tormentors.

Gracious Holy Spirit,
 Thank You for promising to teach me what to say when I need to

defend my faith (Luke 12:11–12).
Make me ever more like You.
Amen.

Pray for others

Find out who needs prayerful and practical support as they suffer persecution. You may find it helpful to contact one of the following organisations:

Release International[14]
Open Doors [15]
Barnabas Fund [16]

21 DEC

Immanuel: Anchoring the soul

'Always winter and never Christmas' describes the bleakness of C.S. Lewis's land of Narnia.[17] No one could change the relentless icescape other than Aslan, the lion king; the only one with the power to bring it new life.

The world provides various means which attempt to alleviate suffering but they will never be sufficient, for as Catherine Campbell writes, 'only the Christ of Christmas is enough to meet those needs'.[18]

Scriptural foundations...
Read Psalm 25

When faced with countless enemies (v.19), David turned to the Lord as his only means of hope and so God responded to his heartfelt cry for protection, guidance and forgiveness. This week, we've considered just a few potential 'enemies' that hound Advent preparations but as we, like David, place all our hope in God, we shall never be beaten down.

The winds of adversity attempt to toss us this way and that, but the hope we have in God's unfailing love, Immanuel's constant presence and an eternity with Him in heaven, anchors the soul securely in the eye of the fiercest storm. Will we choose a winter without Christmas, or will we welcome Immanuel into the bleakness of our trouble and trust Him to restore us with life? Indeed, our eternal hope in Christ's love and presence is '… an anchor for the soul, firm and secure' (Heb. 6:19).

...on which we build

When the angels brought God's message of 'good news of great joy' to the Bethlehem shepherds it didn't alleviate the day to day reality of physical hardships, and the loneliness endured while tending sheep; it didn't increase their lowly status; it didn't miraculously line their pockets with gold; and nor did it release them from the brutality and oppression of Roman occupation. But the message and visitation of Immanuel brought comfort to their hearts and great hope for their future; not by waving a magic wand that changed or eased their circumstances but by His life lived in love, even unto death.

The reality of the gospel message continues to provide God's answer to suffering – not always by alleviating it, but by living in and through the gruelling difficulties, emotional turmoil, hardship, pain and so on. Indeed, His perfect love manifests itself to an imperfect world provided we make room for Him in our hearts to do so. Therein is the strength we need to face today, the hope we can hold on to for tomorrow, and the fulfilment of our inner being no matter where He leads.

Advent Calendar

For digestion: 'He reached down from on high and took hold of me; he drew me out of deep waters' (Psa. 18:16).
For reflection: Picture yourself in a little boat, tackling the storm of your difficulty; hurricane winds whip up walls of water, threatening to crash down right on top of you. Will you frantically attempt paddling to an unknown shore, call out for help although no one can hear you, or use and trust God's refuge and anchor to safely secure you until the storm has passed?

Consider or discuss

- What are you currently hoping for?
- Is your hope based on personal comforts and concerns or God's sovereign purpose?
- Does the answer to your hopes lie with people or Immanuel?

Prayer

'Find rest, O my soul, in God alone;
  my hope comes from him.
He alone is my rock and my salvation;
  he is my fortress,
  I shall not be shaken.
My salvation and my honour depend on God;
  he is my mighty rock,
  my refuge'
Amen.
 (Psa. 62:5–7)

Pray for others

For God's love to flood hopeless hearts,
 For God's peace to calm muddled minds,
 For God's light to shine into life's darkness,
 For God's purpose to heal shattered esteem,
 For Immanuel to anchor the storm-tossed soul.

Coming Together Week 3

Space to talk

Allow time to talk through any issues, queries or helpful inspiration that each group member may have from the daily 'Consider or discuss' questions.

Further discussion...

- Read, then discuss your response to the following quotations:

> It has been said that when life makes no sense, when moments of confusion shred our soul, there are three paths we can take: to abandon any claim to Christian belief and search for immediate relief and happiness; to run from confusion as a woodsman would flee from a hungry bear; or to cling to God with disciplined tenacity, reminding ourselves of who He is, even though our struggle with confusion continues unabated. (Selwyn Hughes)[19]

> The misfortunes of good people are not only a problem to the people who suffer and to their families. They are a problem to everyone who wants to believe in a just and fair and liveable world. They inevitably raise questions about the goodness, the kindness, even the existence of God.' (Harold S. Kushner)[20]

Space to reflect

If you find it helpful, light a candle to focus your busy thoughts on the light of Jesus, then ask someone to read the following passage of Scripture. Spend a few minutes in silence as you consider how God is speaking to you through His living Word today.

> Psalm 42

Space to pray

Pray together:
Pray for the governments, leaders, and the suffering Church in Sudan, Nigeria, Vietnam, China, North Korea, Pakistan and Indonesia – the seven countries suffering most intense Christian persecution, as informed by the Christian Charity, Release International.[21]

Pray for one another:
Pray for each other's difficulties and/or fears for Christmas and the New Year.

Space to worship

Conclude by singing 'Into The Darkness' (Maggi Dawn, 1993 Kingsway's Thankyou Music).

If you do not have musicians in the group, try singing (or listening) to it with a CD/taped accompaniment.

Notes

1. Extract from an article, 'Depression at Christmas' by Dr Trisha Macnair, www.bbc.co.uk/health/
2. An extract from 'Christmas – the heart of the Gospel' by Al Mawhinney, an article of the Reformed Theological Seminary newsletter, Winter 2004. www2.rts.edu
3. Online Office of National Statistics: the number of divorces granted in 2004 was 167,116.
4. Community Care Suicide statistics 9/10/2003.
5. Online Office of National Statistics, Social Trends 33.
6. Homelessness statistics released January 2006; www.ymca.org.uk.
7. Statistic taken from www.samaritans.org.uk on 15 December 2005. Quote from Jeremy Payne, Samaritans' Director of Fundraising and External Relations, from that same website.
8. Alec Motyer, *Tyndale Old Testament Commentaries, Isaiah* (IVP, Leicester, 1999) p.377.
9. Selwyn Hughes, *Every Day With Jesus, 23/12/1990* (CWR, Surrey, 1990).
10. Reported in the *Daily Express* newspaper, Wednesday 16 November 2005.
11. *The Christian Institute Newsletter*, December 2005. After stinging public criticism the council agreed to continue funding the event.
12. *Intercessors for Britain Prayer Bulletin*, Number 200, January/February 2006.
13. Reported in the *Daily Mail* newspaper, 23 December 2005.
14. Release International PO Box 54, Orpington BR5 9RT, tel. 01689 823491.
15. Open Doors PO Box 6, Witney, Oxon OX29 6WG, tel. 01993 885400.
16. Barnabas Fund The Old Rectory, River Street, Pewsey, Wiltshire, SN9 5DB, tel. 08700 603900.
17. See C.S. Lewis, *The Lion, The Witch and The Wardrobe*, (Geoffrey Bles, London, 1950).
18. Catherine Campbell, 'Christmas is not just for the children'; quote from her article published in *Woman Alive* magazine, December 2005.
19. Selwyn Hughes, *Every Day With Jesus, 31/12/1990* (CWR, Surrey, 1990).
20. Harold S. Kushner, *When bad things happen to good people*, (Pan Books, London, 1982) p.14–15.
21. Box 54, Orpington BR5 9RT, www.releaseinternational.org

WEEK FOUR

The Ethos of Immanuel

22 DEC

The ethos of life in His presence

Although there are just three days left of the traditional Advent period, the repercussions are ongoing; learning to live with Immanuel's presence every hour of each day. It reminds me of the tribe of Levi who were set apart to minister as priests before God's presence (Exod. 32:29; Deut. 10:8); their clothing, training, tasks and inheritance distinguishing them from the people.

Similarly, as we learn to live in God's presence, we too shall be set apart; distinctive by the ethos of Lord Immanuel.

Scriptural foundations...

Read Haggai 2:1–9

Clearing rubble and attempting to rebuild God's ransacked residence in Jerusalem, the returned exiles grew disheartened, for their lack of adequate resources and manpower prevented them from emulating its magnificent predecessor. Seeing their distress, God sent His word of encouragement through Haggai the prophet.

The Israelites were building a temple of stone but One would come and fill it with glory far surpassing anything that humankind could manufacture. Haggai described Jesus as 'the desired of all nations' – He was the Person everyone had been waiting for, whether or not they realised or believed it.

As post-resurrection believers we've the awesome privilege of knowing the glorious riches of our salvation, '… which is Christ in [us], the hope of glory' (Col. 1:27). Now is the time to put that privilege into practice; to experience the reality of living with the richness and glory of Christ's presence.

...on which we build

'God has made us in such a way that we only become really human when we are in harmony with his life and love. His will, his presence, his personal being is indeed what we most deeply want' (Dr Rowan Williams).[1]

There are many self-help books currently available – how to achieve promotion, increase our self-worth, find purpose in life, and so on. But the reality of putting Dr Williams' thought-provoking statement into practice and achieving the fulfilled life Jesus promised (John 10:10), requires more than theological head knowledge. Rather, it develops with an ever-increasing awareness of living our lives in the presence of Almighty God.

With my daughter engaged and away at university, my home at this time in 2005 felt somewhat empty and sad. Filled with nostalgic memories of my own childhood Christmases and with my family out of reach in Guernsey, I began to feel so homesick. Sitting on the sofa sobbing with the Lord, my thoughts turned to this book. Silly old me! It wasn't about who would appreciate my nativity scene or creative handiwork – it was all about Jesus breathing life into it all.

The ethos of Immanuel doesn't come from belief alone, but by recognising and engaging with the presence of His Spirit. Who better to guide us this week than some of the people involved with His first coming: Zechariah, Joseph, Mary, shepherds, Simeon, Anna and the Magi.

Advent Calendar

For digestion: 'My heart says of you, "Seek his face!" Your face, LORD, I will seek' (Psa. 27:8).

For reflection: Picture the scene of your usual waking routines. How long does it take before you acknowledge that God is with you?

Consider or discuss

'Man's chief and highest end is to glorify God, and fully to enjoy Him forever' (from the Westminster Catechism).

- Consider the implications of this statement – to what degree is it true to your life?

Prayer

I AM WHO I AM.

You are Who you are;
You are God – Almighty, Sovereign, Omniscient, Omnipresent – and You are with me.
The mysteries of salvation, the power of resurrection, the purposes of time itself,
are with me.
The light of Your presence, the comfort of Your love, the richness of Your beauty,
are with me.
Father, Son and Holy Spirit,
I acknowledge You within my heart;
Glorify Your presence through my life,
now and for ever.
Amen.

Pray for others

Pray for children taking part in nativity plays that through their practice and performance they may find greater understanding of the true message of Christmas.

23 DEC

Zechariah: The ethos of prayer

Imagine trying to live with someone but barely, if ever, communicating. Inevitably an edgy atmosphere develops which might eventually lead to a breakdown of relationship. The result would be no different if we lived like that with Immanuel.

Thus we're urged to develop some clear and well-used channels of communication, and our finest tool for doing so is prayer.

Scriptural foundations...

Read Luke 1:5–25

Being chosen to burn incense in the Holy Place, right in front of the veiled Most Holy Place of God's presence, was a once in a lifetime privilege. As the priests prepared to lead the people in prayer outside the sanctuary, the one who'd been chosen entered alone and waited for the signal. As soon as he heard it, he sprinkled fragrant incense onto the burning coals atop a golden altar; then priests and people began to pray.

It was during this scenario that an angel of the Lord appeared to Zechariah with the message concerning his wife's pregnancy – that which would fulfil Isaiah's prophetic expectancy of the one who'd prepare the way for the Lord (Isa. 40:3). Zechariah had lived a devout and godly life, and although he was never permitted entry into the Most Holy Place of God's presence (an entitlement restricted for the high priest, just once a year), his responsibilities as a priest in God's house trained him how to live prayerfully within His close proximity.

...on which we build

We are now part of a holy priesthood in Christ Jesus (1 Pet. 2:5–9), and have the privilege of entering God's presence for ourselves, bringing the fragrance of reverent prayer at any time of day or night. Are we making use of that wonderful privilege or does busyness, apathy or other desires, distract us from talking with God?

Paul said, 'pray continually' (1 Thess. 5:17) because prayer isn't meant to be merely set aside for when we are in church or for during our devotions. As important and essential as that form of prayer is, it's designed to accompany us throughout the day and thereby develop awareness of Immanuel's constant presence.

This was a reality expressed through the life of the seventeenth-century monk, Brother Lawrence: 'It was, he said, enormous self-deception to believe that the time of prayer must be different from any other. We are equally bound to be one with God by what we do in times of action as by the time of prayer at its special hour. His prayer was simply the presence of God, his soul unconscious of all else but love.'[2]

Advent Calendar

For digestion: 'May my prayer be set before you like incense; may the lifting up of my hands be like the evening sacrifice' (Psa. 141:2).
For reflection: Picture yourself praying. Is it composed of just one image or many?

Consider or discuss

- How often do you commune with God during an average twenty-four-hour day?
- Do you find the Advent and Christmas period inspires you to pray more, or less?
- In what variety of ways do you enjoy communing with Immanuel? How would you like to develop this?
- Even during the last minute rush to prepare for Christmas Day, opportunities arise for prayer. For example, rather than feeling frustrated by extended time in queues, you may like to use the opportunity to talk with God.

Prayer

Lord Jesus, you exemplified a life of constant communion with Your Father. Teach me how to do likewise. Amen.

Pray for others

Immanuel, the Great Shepherd of God's flock,
we thank You for those men and women that You have ordained to assist You;
who lead us, teach us, pray for us, encourage us and care for us.
Thank You for their willing self-sacrifice in order to serve us,
and for the love You've placed in their hearts for us,
even when we're not always easy to love!
Amen.

24 DEC

Joseph: The ethos of obedience

The proposal was as romantic as a girl could ever have dreamt, standing beneath floodlit Parisian fountains one balmy summer's night. But in saying 'yes' to becoming his wife, I also said 'yes' to becoming his six-year-old's second mother.

As tragic as her first mother's death had been some years before, God prepared my heart and hers for a unique, loving relationship that I wouldn't swap for anyone. Nevertheless, the memory of those initial adjustments to married life accompanied by immediate motherhood, arouse special empathy for Joseph's discreet yet essential role in the boyhood years of Jesus.

Scriptural foundations...
Read Matthew 1:18–25

Joseph and Mary were pledged to be married; a contract that could only be broken through death or divorce. And divorce it might well have been had Joseph followed his initial reaction to the news of her untimely pregnancy.

It certainly wasn't the scenario Joseph had hoped for his engagement; reeling with wretched desolation from her seeming betrayal and rebuff. But he didn't erupt with irrational behaviour on the basis of human reaction, and that precious time taken to consider his dilemma provided space for the Lord to speak, and the strength for him to obey.

Fathering a child conceived in his prospective wife by another was by no means an easy task for Joseph to accept – angelic messenger or not. He had to rely on God to dispel any seeds of mistrust and let go of the shattered 'what could have been' dreams, revering God's ways as far higher than his feelings, His thoughts far greater than human purpose.

...on which we build
Sometimes I wonder if my faith and commitment would be further

enhanced if God revealed His will as clearly as He did to Joseph. In reality, however, I know that I'll always find reasons to satisfy my own inclinations if that's where my heart really lies. In fact, I believe God does speak clearly about His purposes, but the question lies with how willing I am to listen, believe, accept and obey – especially when the task requires considerable self-sacrifice of my reputation, time, aspirations, comforts, finance and so on.

In developing our awareness of life in God's presence we may need to improve our listening skills, but no matter how well we hear Him we have to be willing to obey. Such is the challenge from Joseph's life now awaiting our response.

Advent Calendar

For digestion: '… "Be strong and courageous, and do the work. Do not be afraid or discouraged, for the LORD God, my God, is with you…"' (1 Chron. 28:20).

For reflection: Imagine kneeling before God's majestic throne waiting for His instructions. But have you pinned any labels to your heart, negotiating conditions or parameters before you'll submit and obey?

Consider or discuss

So, my dear friends, listen carefully;
 those who embrace these my ways are most blessed.
Mark a life of discipline and live wisely;
 don't squander your precious life.
Blessed the man, blessed the woman, who listens to me,
 awake and ready for me each morning,
 alert and responsive as I start my day's work.
When you find me, you find life, real life,
 to say nothing of God's good pleasure.
  (Prov. 8:33–35, *The Message*)

Prayer

Lord, I've been kneeling here for a long time and I still perceive an unwillingness to trust and obey Your purposes without knowing what You might ask.

Forgive my endless list of, 'what ifs?';

Please grant me the ability to hear You clearly
and Your strength when mine is failing, to help me to obey.
Amen.

Pray for others

Lord, I pray for those who've left home or wife or brothers or parents or children for the sake of Your kingdom (*name some if you can*). Grant them today, the blessing of Your tangible presence and a portion of the reward that You promised for them in this life. Give them also great comfort, joy and satisfaction as they await their reward in heaven.

(Based on Luke 18:29–30)

25 DEC

Mary: The ethos of joy

> Joy to the world! the Lord has come; Let earth receive her King.
> Let every heart prepare Him room, And heaven and nature sing …
> Isaac Watts, 1674–1748

May I send you my warmest greetings for a Happy Christmas, filled with the joy of Immanuel – God with us – living in your heart.

Scriptural foundations...
Read Luke 1:46–55; 2:1–7

As the realisation of Whom she was carrying increasingly dawned upon Mary, her soul overflowed with joy. And how inordinately happy she felt nine months later as her firstborn was placed in her arms.

Feelings, however, no matter how euphoric, inevitably fluctuate. She wouldn't have felt 'full of the joys' when faced with public disgrace nor, as heavily pregnant, she undertook an arduous journey to endure the rigours of childbirth without bed or privacy. Nor would she have felt happy when her godly husband died, nor perhaps when Jesus included others in the intimate love of mother and son (Matt. 12:48–49), and certainly not as she stood by helplessly, watching Him die at the hands of cruel tormentors.

Feelings of happiness, however, cannot compare to the joy of the Holy Spirit. Such is the depth and reality of His joy that it lingers to sustain us despite how we may feel. Indeed, the joy of the Lord God was the strength Jesus needed to face and endure the terror of His death (Heb. 12:2); the fullness of joy through the Holy Spirit made available to us through His resurrection.

...on which we build

We can feel joy in pleasing circumstances, and perhaps today you feel happiness arising from a celebratory service at church, gatherings with family or friends, or the exchanging of gifts, the pleasures of fine food, and so on.

Moreover, we can choose to rejoice in response to scriptural promises (Phil. 4:4). No matter how we feel today, the truth is that we're remembering God's mission to grant us eternal life – we might, therefore, choose through faith to partake in joyful celebrations.

Nevertheless, the innate joy of the fruit of the Holy Spirit (Gal. 5:22) finds expression as we nurture our relationship with Immanuel. Some of us may feel anything but 'happy' this Christmas Day, but the more we seek an awareness of His presence, the more we shall share and find renewed strength in His eternal joy.

I am praying for you today, that you may be restored with the joy of His salvation (Psa. 51:12) – the unbeatable gift of Christmas.

Advent Calendar

For digestion: 'For the kingdom of God is not a matter of eating and drinking, but of righteousness, peace and joy in the Holy Spirit' (Rom. 14:17).

For reflection: Picture a white chrysanthemum placed in a vase of pink dye. The more of the dye it drinks through its stem, the pinker its petals become. The more we experience Immanuel, the greater the abundance of His joy.

Consider or discuss

- What makes you feel happy, or otherwise, on Christmas Day?
- Have you experienced the promised joy of Immanuel?

- What joy can you perceive with the help of the Spirit to help you face your 'cross'?

Prayer

O holy Child of Bethlehem,
Descend to us, we pray;
Cast out our sin, and enter in;
Be born in us today.
We hear the Christmas angels
The great glad tidings tell;
O come to us, abide with us,
Our Lord Immanuel!
Phillips Brooks, 1835–93

Pray for others

Immanuel, who came to be with us on Christmas Day;
for those whose hours are filled with suffering or bereavement,
for those who are far from home, without family or friends,
for those who are wracked with pain or mental illness,
for those who will be working to serve our human needs,
bring to them, we pray, the incomparable joy of experiencing Your presence.
Amen.

26 DEC

Shepherds: The ethos of personal testimony

Having hurried to Bethlehem, the result of being in Jesus' presence sent shepherds scurrying throughout the neighbourhood to tell others of their newfound knowledge. Is that what scribes would write about our own encounter with Christ?

Scriptural foundations...

Read Luke 2:8–20

The shepherds weren't educated scholars, theological geniuses or great orators, but from hearing the message and meeting Jesus for themselves, their immediate response was to go tell other people (Luke 2:17).

Hearing or reading about someone may have an influence upon our lives, but it's only by meeting them personally that their impact has greatest effect. In fact, the shepherds had a fantastic tale to tell when relating the angelic message, but meeting Jesus gave credence to a story that might otherwise be dismissed as the effects of too much fireside wine!

So, let's 'hurry' to be with Jesus, to engage our minds and hearts with Immanuel, for the impact of a life lived in His presence provides endless reasons to tell others all about Him.

...on which we build

Imagine being asked to give a testimony in church next week about how you've engaged with God recently. What have you been learning about His character and ways, what has He been showing and teaching you, or in what ways has He disciplined, encouraged, challenged, healed or comforted you? Would you be willing to stand up and share – and how would you respond if subsequently asked to do this every Sunday for a year?

I confess I'd be tempted to make excuses as I'm naturally shy and often find it difficult to express myself in words (preferring to do so through writing!). Living with the constant, daily awareness of the Lord Jesus Christ, however, far surpasses human limitations. Moses and Paul weren't gifted orators but neither could they help themselves from relating their experiences.

Some of us might decline, however, because we simply had nothing to say. If so, let's use the mere thought of being accountable at church to inspire us to live in the life-changing presence of God.

Advent Calendar

For digestion: 'Jesus left that place and went to the vicinity of Tyre. He entered a house and did not want anyone to know it; yet he could not keep his presence secret' (Mark 7:24).

For reflection: Take a look at your life, work and ministry in the church – and also at your relationships with non-believers. The more you live with the awareness of Immanuel, the less you'll be able to keep His presence secret! To what extent is He already being made known through your life?

Consider or discuss

- What would prevent you from sharing a testimony with a non-believer: embarrassment or fear of rejection?
- What would prevent you from giving a testimony in church: shyness or simply having nothing to say?
- What would have happened if no one had ever shared their testimony with you?
- What difference would it make to your life if you'd never had the opportunity to be inspired or encouraged by the testimony of other believers?

Prayer

The angels guided the shepherds to Your birthplace as the star guided the Magi; and You, Yourself were a magnetic personality as You walked the land of Israel. Lord, Immanuel, guide others to Your presence by the light and power of my personal testimony. Amen.

Pray for others

First pray that God will give you favour, as He did for Joseph (Gen. 39:21), in the eyes and hearts of those to whom you speak. Then pray that they will respond to the inspiration of the message that you share: '... Always be prepared to give an answer to everyone who asks you to give the reason for the hope that you have. But do this with gentleness and respect' (1 Pet. 3:15).

27 DEC

Simeon and Anna: The ethos of the Word

Jesus and the Word are synonymous, for 'In the beginning was the Word, and the Word was with God, and the Word was God. ... The Word became flesh and made his dwelling among us. ... the glory of the One and Only, who came from the Father, full of grace and truth' (John 1:1,14).

Scriptural foundations...
Read Luke 2:21–40

For any Israelite man to earn the title 'righteous and devout' or any woman to 'never [leave] the temple' suggests they'd acquired a deep knowledge of God's Word – further enhanced by the length of years they'd absorbed it into their hearts.

Forty days after giving birth, Mary fulfilled her obligation to Mosaic Law and, with Joseph, presented her offering of purification in the Temple (Lev. 12:6–8); restoring as she did so, the glory of God's presence in the form of a tiny baby. Indeed, God's *Shekinah* glory that graced Solomon's Temple had never appeared in Herod's, but Simeon and Anna recognised the fulfilment of prophecy through Jesus – salvation, light and glory to all people (Isa. 40:3–5; 49:6).

...on which we build
In the Western world we're generally able to afford at least one Bible, and at the time of writing we still have our freedom to read it without breaking the law. But do we read it, and if so, how often? How important is regular Bible study and meditation in our twenty-four-hour routine? Do we perceive it as a dusty tome of dos, don'ts and difficult theology, or have we given space for Immanuel to bring it alive to our souls, just as He did for our aged Temple friends? Indeed, 'the word of God is living and active. Sharper than any double-edged sword, it penetrates even to dividing soul and spirit, joints and marrow; it judges the thoughts and attitudes of the heart' (Heb. 4:12).

Although we're not solely reliant on the Bible to meet with God and be filled with His Spirit, He's written it to help us live with Him and learn of His holy ways; an unbeatable handbook for life and reference for our devotions.

Advent Calendar

For digestion: 'My son, keep my words and store up my commands within you. Keep my commands and you will live; guard my teachings as the apple of your eye. Bind them on your fingers; write them on the tablet of your heart' (Prov. 7:1–3).
For reflection: Take a look at your Bible if you have one. How well do you know its contents? Is it like a close friend you long to share with daily, or a sporadic acquaintance you barely know or understand?

Consider or discuss

- If you misplaced your Bible, how long would it take before you noticed?
- If the law of the land confiscated your Bible, how much would you already have stored within your heart?

Prayer

Immanuel – Word made flesh now living in my heart,
'How sweet are your words to my taste, sweeter than honey to my mouth!' (Psa. 119:103); teaching my heart, nourishing my soul with Your precious bread of life.

Immanuel –
'Your word is a lamp to my feet and a light for my path' (Psa. 119:105); guide my steps in Your paths of truth.

Immanuel –
'... the word of God ... judges the thoughts and attitudes of the heart' (Heb. 4:12); purge my life of all ungodliness and refill it with Your loving goodness.

Immanuel –
'You are my refuge and my shield; I have put my hope in your

word' (Psa. 119:114); protect, defend and guard my life with Your divine power and might.

Immanuel – Word made flesh now living in my heart.
Amen.

Pray for others
Pray for the work of Wycliffe International and the Bible Society whose team of linguists and missionaries translate Scripture into thousands of languages worldwide.

Pray for the people who speak one of 4,500 languages who have yet to receive just one book of the Bible translated into their tongue.[3]

28 DEC

Magi: The ethos of worship

'Bring to Me, the Christ-child, your gifts, truly the gifts of earth's wisest.
The Gold – your money.
Frankincense – the adoration of a consecrated life.
Myrrh – your sharing in My sorrows and those of the world.'[4]

Scriptural foundations...
Read Matthew 2:1–12

The Magi, or wise men from the East, were the first Gentiles to publicly acknowledge Jesus was King – and this they did through worship. Jesus came for all people, to be worshipped by all people; that was and is His right as King.

My dictionary defines worship as showing 'profound religious devotion and respect; to adore or venerate',[5] and both the Old Testament Hebrew and New Testament Greek teach us how:

> '*shachah* (Gen. 22:5) – to depress ie prostrate (… in homage to royalty or God): bow (self) down … do (make) obeisance, do reverence, make to stoop …'[6]

> '*proskuneo* (Matt. 2:11) – to fawn or crouch, to prostrate oneself in homage (do reverence to, adore).'[7]

From the moment they set out on their star-led journey, the Magi had one thing in mind, to worship a newborn king. That was the sole intent and purpose of travelling hundreds of miles (Matt. 2:2). They could not worship from a distance, they had to be in His presence; and the moment they were, they bowed down, worshipped and presented Him with gifts. 'Did the Magi realise that the baby lying before them would change the nature of worship forever?' (Selwyn Hughes).[8]

...on which we build

The overriding purpose of seeking God's presence is to worship Him – to prostrate our 'self' in submission to His Lordship, to honour, revere and adore Him, to present to Him the gifts of our lives.

Living with an increasing awareness of Immanuel highlights the ongoing nature of worship. It's no longer restricted to stables or temples, nor is it merely the weekly singing in church. Worship is a way of life for those of us seeking the reality of Immanuel – a life of sacrifice, submission, reverence and service to God living with us; the result of prayerfully seeking Him with all of our heart.

We do not worship for what we can get, but for what we can give – everything that we have, everything that we are, and everything that we experience, in reverence of Almighty God.

And that is the ethos of a life lived in His presence.

Advent Calendar

For digestion: 'God is spirit, and his worshippers must worship in spirit and in truth' (John 4:24).
For reflection: Picture yourself worshipping God – where are you and what are you doing?

Consider or discuss

- Where or what do you see as your place of worship? How could you expand this?
- What do you see yourself giving to God in worship? What more could you offer?

- How might you develop an ethos of worship, 24/7?

Prayer

Make time today to express a prayer of worship to God in some way other than singing or praying with words.

Pray for others

Pray for those who perceive the Lord far off, but do not draw near to worship.

Pray for those who have acknowledged His presence, but do not desire to worship.

Pray for those who once bowed their hearts and wills in worship, but who've now lost sight of the One they once adored.

Coming Together Week 4

Space to talk

Allow time to talk through any issues, queries or helpful inspiration that each group member may have from the daily 'Consider or discuss' questions.

Further discussion...

On 23 December 2005, an acquaintance of mine sat in the café of a high street retailer, sipping coffee while girding herself up to lunge into the packed hall of shoppers. A woman heaved past, pushing a trolley on the brink of shedding its gargantuan load with a toddler kicking and screaming to get out from its seat.

It was only 8am.

'Is this what Christmas has come to?' she pondered, as she watched them disappear behind a mountain of tinned biscuits …

- How would you respond to her question?
- Perhaps enjoy some seasonal refreshments and relax and talk over how you've been challenged or inspired to 'practise the presence of God'.

Space to reflect

If you find it helpful, light a candle to focus your busy thoughts on the light of Jesus, then ask someone to read the following passage of Scripture. Spend a few minutes in silence as you consider how God is speaking to you through His living Word today.

Psalm 139:7–18

Space to pray

Pray together:

Praise God for Christmas.
Praise Him for the Incarnation
for Word made flesh.
I will not sing
of shepherds watching flocks
on frosty night or angel choristers.
I will not sing of stable bare in Bethlehem or lowing oxen
wise men
trailing distant star
with gold and frankincense and myrrh.
Tonight I will sing
praise to the Father
who stood on heaven's threshold
and said farewell to His Son
as He stepped across the stars
to Bethlehem
and Jerusalem.
And I will sing praise to the infinite eternal Son
who became most finite a Baby
who would one day be executed
for my crimes.
Praise Him in the heavens.
Praise Him in the stable.
Praise Him in my heart.

Joseph Bayly – A Psalm for Christmas Eve[9]

Pray for one another:
Pray in a group or in pairs that throughout the new year, each person would develop a greater awareness of the presence of Immanuel throughout every day.

Space to worship

Conclude by singing 'All To Jesus I Surrender' (J.W. van de Venter, 1855–1939).

If you do not have musicians in the group, try singing (or listening) to it with a CD/taped accompaniment.

Notes

1. Christmas message from the Archbishop of Canterbury 22/12/2003.
2. Brother Lawrence, *The Practice of the Presence of God* (Hodder & Stoughton, London, 1981) p.29.
3. The Bible Society.
4. *God Calling* by The Two Listeners (Arthur James Ltd, Suffolk, 1953, reprinted 1991) p.280.
5. Patrick Hanks (ed.), *Collins Dictionary of the English Language* (Glasgow: William Collins, 1979).
6. Strong's 7812 (Strong's Electronic Concordance KJV Copyright 1989 © Tristar Publishing).
7. Strong's 4352 (Strong's Electronic Concordance KJV Copyright 1989 © Tristar Publishing).
8. Selwyn Hughes, *Every Day with Jesus*, 'Fresh Vision for Worship', Sep/Oct 2003.
9. Joseph Bayly, material from *Psalms of My Life* (David C. Cook Publishing Co., Elgin IL, 1987). Used by permission of Kingsway UK Publishing.

WEEK FIVE

Immanuel is Coming Again

29 DEC

Are you ready?

In just three days, further festivities and fireworks will announce another year, one that may hold promise for new job opportunities, relationships, ministries and so on – provided Jesus doesn't come back first!

Scriptural foundations...
Read Matthew 24:36 – 25:13

Today's opening verse narrates Jesus' response to the disciples' question in Matthew 24:3 and launches a discussion about the unknown time of His return, concluding at 25:13. The overriding implication of each parable is to be ready – moreover, to maintain a constant readiness 'because you do not know on what day your Lord will come' (24:42).

Jesus was preparing the disciples for a long wait (24:48; 25:5). Indeed, it's already been more than 2,000 years since Christ's first Advent, a time span that may induce apathy concerning His return. Being ready doesn't simply mean repenting then waiting, but serving and providing for others in ways that we've each been asked to (24:45).

He will come back suddenly, 'in a flash, in the twinkling of an eye' (1 Cor. 15:52), and just when we're least expecting Him. Are we ready? Will He know us? Will we be doing His work? No one else's readiness can prepare us for that day (Matt. 25:6–10).

...on which we build

If you knew when Jesus was coming back, would it affect what you're doing today? What difference would it make if you knew He would return in ten days, ten hours, ten minutes, ten seconds? What confession would you make or relationships put right, and who would you want to tell?

We've spent considerable time this month preparing to live with Immanuel, so I trust that we're ready to meet our Maker face to face. Nevertheless, our passage repeats the all-important question. Are we ready for Christ's second coming? If not, we may suddenly find the time has come and gone and won't be able to turn back the clock. Furthermore, Jesus' commission was to make disciples, not just believers. Are we guiding and encouraging each other in the ways of our Lord, serving one another with the gifts we've been given to do so?

As we turn our backs on this year let's not lose sight of Immanuel. Let's keep the reality of 'God with us' alive through every day, while faithfully fulfilling His work.

Advent Calendar

For digestion: 'He who testifies to these things says, "Yes, I am coming soon." Amen. Come, Lord Jesus' (Rev. 22:20).
For reflection: Picture a celebratory feast filled with fine food, radiant faces, love, laughter and vibrant life. Can you see your face among the guests? Who is outside banging frantically on the door, but unable to come in?

Consider or discuss

- What would be your response if Jesus appeared with you right now?
- If you are enjoying youth or good health, you may not think too much about death. But none of us knows when God will take us from this world, and if Jesus doesn't return beforehand, then the moment you step out of time into eternity will be the moment you're called to account …
- … so too for your family and friends.

Prayer
Lord, Immanuel, while I know that in myself, I'll never be perfectly ready to meet You, may no task be left undone, no word left unsaid, no person missing the divine touch that You planned for them through my life. Amen.

Pray for others
Pray for Christian friends who've lost sight of the second coming. Pray for the Spirit to reignite their passion and zeal for that day.

30 DEC

Are they ready?

The perceived eccentricities of John the Baptist may be seen in modern alternatives; someone, for example, sporting billboards proclaiming, 'The end is nigh!' But no matter how these heralds appear, we too have a part to play in discharging their message and mission.

Scriptural foundations...
Read Isaiah 40:1–11

Isaiah's message of comfort with its tender image of the shepherd gently caring for his flock, contrasts significantly with the coarse-clothed, locust-eating, passionate preacher John. But John the Baptist's voice it was which Isaiah foretold would prepare the way for the Lord (Matt. 3:3).

John had a message with a mission:

His message – 'Repent, for the kingdom of heaven is near' (Matt. 3:2).

His mission – 'to make ready a people prepared for the Lord' (Luke 1:17).

'*Repent* means more than 'be sorry' or even 'change your mind'; it echoes the Old Testament prophets' frequent summons to Israel to 'return' to God, to abandon rebellion and come back into covenant-obedience.'[1] Thus, John made ready a people who were prepared to meet Jesus, their Saviour, in person.

Confessing our sin and turning back to God's holy ways still prepares a level path for His coming to us. And what a coming it will be when, 'the glory of the LORD will be revealed' (Isa. 40:5); 'the fullness of His personal presence.'[2]

...on which we build

Yesterday we read how 'being ready' ourselves includes a responsibility to other people – like a two-sided coin, you can't have one without the other (Matt. 24:45; 28:19–20). We're all stewards of God's kingdom; each of us gifted and equipped to share Him with others.

John's message bore two slants. Firstly, he captured the tender essence of a voice calling out in the desert, offering God's consolation to those, as it were, in exile from His presence. Secondly, to the 'brood of vipers' (Matt. 3:1–10), the hypocrites who relied on religious ceremony to win divine favour, he lashed out with God's wrath.

And so we're encouraged to speak tenderly to the exiles of our own generation, to the people living far away from God; to woo them with His love and reassure them of His forgiveness if only they'd repent and turn back to their heavenly Father. Tragically, however, the wrath of God's judgment awaits those who continually deny their need of a Saviour or rely on mere ritual and head knowledge.

Ours is to bring the message to an unsaved generation – theirs is the choice to receive or reject it.

Advent Calendar

For digestion: 'How, then, can they call on the one they have not believed in? And how can they believe in the one of whom they have not heard? And how can they hear without someone preaching to them?' (Rom. 10:14)

For reflection: Bring to mind the familiar faces of friends and family whom you've not told about Jesus. What would their last words be to you if Jesus returned today?

Consider or discuss

- In what ways could you share the tenderness of God's call to 'exiles' that you know?
- Condemning your friends as a 'brood of vipers' will hardly win them over to Christ; but how might God be inspiring you to share this part of His message?

Prayer

'... to make ready a people prepared for the Lord' (Luke 1:17).

How can I ever do that Lord
but by Your presence with me, empowering me for my tasks;
but by Your Spirit in me, transforming my sinful heart;
but by Your voice calling out though mine to the needs of this barren world.
Whatever the cost,
whomever the people,
wherever You wish to send me,
use me, I pray, to make ready many people for the day they will meet You as returning King.
Amen.

Pray for others

Make a list of everyone you know personally who is not ready to meet Jesus, then as part of your commitment to pray for them, consider the different ways you might further befriend them, love them and so share Immanuel with them.

31 DEC

Immanuel into the New Year

'He must become greater; I must become less' (John 3:30), was the hallmark of a life committed to making ready a people prepared to meet the Lord. And so, as we conclude our December reflection, may Immanuel become increasingly greater as we give Him more space in our lives.

Scriptural foundations...

Read Titus 2:1 – 3:2

Writing to this potential church leader, Paul highlighted the importance of encouraging self-controlled lives. Admittedly he dispersed such godly qualities amongst their social order, but his use of 'likewise' and 'similarly' reiterate his teaching's relevance to all to whom the grace of God has come (v.11).

Whether or not we think of ourselves as leaders, and no matter our age, sex, marital status, occupation or role in the church and society, as Christian believers we all have potential to influence, lead and therefore teach others about God – not by might nor by power, but by the Spirit of Immanuel, living in our hearts (Zech. 4:6). We've already considered the quality of our personal Advent advert, and now in preparing for Christ's second coming we're reminded to 'make the teaching about God our Saviour attractive' (2:10).

...on which we build

Jesus' powerful personality and teaching drew massive crowds from far afield. The attraction wasn't just what He said, it was also the way that He lived His life – a heart that welled with compassion for the poor, the lonely and rejected; hands that touched the untouchables with loving acceptance; eyes that shone with the security of self-worth founded in God; a demeanour that reverenced the divine.

This Jesus lives in the heart of every believer; Immanuel – God with us. Nevertheless, we still have the choice to allow His Spirit increasing measure of influence in and through our lives.

'My life is my message,' declared Mahatma Gandhi.[3] As we stand on the doorstep of a new year, let's commit ourselves to the message and Lordship of Immanuel, so that in every way we will make Him attractive to others.

Advent Calendar

For digestion: 'Watch your life and doctrine closely. Persevere in them, because if you do, you will save both yourself and your hearers' (1 Tim. 4:16).

For reflection: Picture the transformation and changes that may occur in your life in the next twelve months as you align it to

Immanuel. Keep hold of this vision when circumstances may entice you from following His ways.

Consider or discuss

In his New Year's message for 2006, Conservative Party leader, David Cameron, reminded members and supporters that, '… personal commitment is the most powerful way to bring about change.'[4]

- What changes has God been inspiring for your life this year?
- How committed are you to allowing Him to bring about that change as you submit to His will and His ways?

Declare in faith for yourself and others…

> … we do not preach ourselves, but Jesus Christ as Lord, and ourselves as your servants for Jesus' sake. For God, who said, "Let light shine out of darkness," made his light shine in our hearts to give us the light of the knowledge of the glory of God in the face of Christ.
>
> But we have this treasure in jars of clay to show that this all-surpassing power is from God and not from us. We are hard pressed on every side, but not crushed; perplexed, but not in despair; persecuted, but not abandoned; struck down, but not destroyed. We always carry around in our body the death of Jesus, so that the life of Jesus may also be revealed in our body … So we fix our eyes not on what is seen, but on what is unseen. For what is seen is temporary, but what is unseen is eternal. Amen.
>
> (2 Cor. 4:5–10,18)

Notes

1. R.T. France, *Tyndale New Testament Commentaries, Matthew* (IVP, Leicester, 1985) p.90.
2. A. Motyer, *Tyndale Old Testament Commentaries, Isaiah* (IVP, Leicester, 1999) p.244.
3. Indian philosopher, statesman and nationalist leader, 1869–1948. According to newspaper/websites, Ghandi was once asked by a reporter 'What is your message?', and his response was 'My life is my message.'
4. Quoted in the *Daily Telegraph*, Saturday 31 December 2005.

National Distributors

UK: (and countries not listed below)
CWR, Waverley Abbey House, Waverley Lane, Farnham, Surrey GU9 8EP.
Tel: (01252) 784700 Outside UK (+44) 1252 784700

AUSTRALIA: CMC Australasia, PO Box 519, Belmont, Victoria 3216.
Tel: (03) 5241 3288 Fax: (03) 5241 3290

CANADA: Cook Communications Ministries, PO Box 98, 55 Woodslee Avenue, Paris, Ontario N3L 3E5.
Tel: 1800 263 2664

GHANA: Challenge Enterprises of Ghana, PO Box 5723, Accra.
Tel: (021) 222437/223249 Fax: (021) 226227

HONG KONG: Cross Communications Ltd, 1/F, 562A Nathan Road, Kowloon.
Tel: 2780 1188 Fax: 2770 6229

INDIA: Crystal Communications, 10-3-18/4/1, East Marredpalli, Secunderabad – 500026, Andhra Pradesh.
Tel/Fax: (040) 27737145

KENYA: Keswick Books and Gifts Ltd, PO Box 10242, Nairobi.
Tel: (02) 331692/226047 Fax: (02) 728557

MALAYSIA: Salvation Book Centre (M) Sdn Bhd, 23 Jalan SS 2/64, 47300 Petaling Jaya, Selangor.
Tel: (03) 78766411/78766797 Fax: (03) 78757066/78756360

NEW ZEALAND: CMC Australasia, PO Box 36015, Lower Hutt.
Tel: 0800 449 408 Fax: 0800 449 049

NIGERIA: FBFM, Helen Baugh House, 96 St Finbarr's College Road, Akoka, Lagos.
Tel: (01) 7747429/4700218/825775/827264

PHILIPPINES: OMF Literature Inc, 776 Boni Avenue, Mandaluyong City.
Tel: (02) 531 2183 Fax: (02) 531 1960

SINGAPORE: Armour Publishing Pte Ltd, Block 203A Henderson Road,
11–06 Henderson Industrial Park, Singapore 159546.
Tel: 6 276 9976 Fax: 6 276 7564

SOUTH AFRICA: Struik Christian Books, 80 MacKenzie Street, PO Box 1144, Cape Town 8000.
Tel: (021) 462 4360 Fax: (021) 461 3612

SRI LANKA: Christombu Publications (Pvt) Ltd, Bartlett House, 65 Braybrooke Place, Colombo 2.
Tel: (01) 433142/328909

TANZANIA: CLC Christian Book Centre, PO Box 1384, Mkwepu Street, Dar es Salaam.
Tel/Fax: (022) 2119439

USA: Cook Communications Ministries, PO Box 98, 55 Woodslee Avenue, Paris, Ontario N3L 3E5, Canada.
Tel: 1800 263 2664

ZIMBABWE: Word of Life Books (Pvt) Ltd, Christian Media Centre, 8 Aberdeen Road, Avondale,
PO Box A480 Avondale, Harare.
Tel: (04) 333355 or 091301188

For email addresses, visit the CWR website: www.cwr.org.uk

CWR is a registered charity – Number 294387

CWR is a limited company registered in England – Registration Number 1990308

CWR
Crusade for World Revival
Applying God's Word to everyday life and relationships

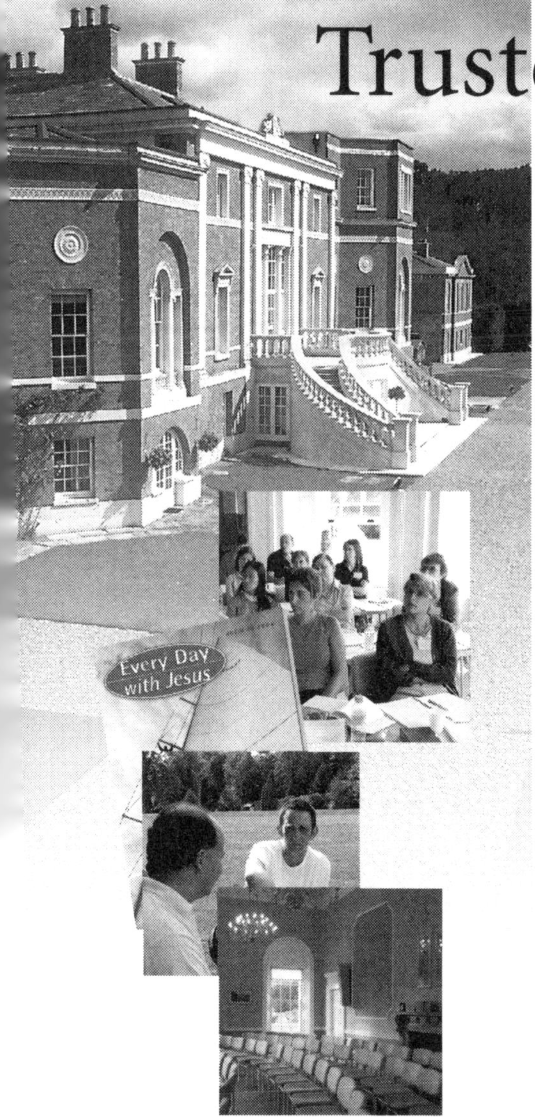

Advent Joy

Elizabeth Rundle

These daily devotions for December seek to recapture the true joy of Jesus' birth through the study of biblical characters, hymns, prayers, Christian testimony and personal observations.

Each day has a Bible reading, a meditation and points for discussion or consideration.

For individual or group use.

£6.99 (plus p&p)

ISBN-10: 1-85345-356-0
ISBN-13: 978-1-85345-356-4

A Journey through Advent

Rob Frost

A thought-provoking book in a daily format, designed to help Christians make their own journey with some of the key characters of the Advent season.

As you walk alongside them you will be strengthened and encouraged in the journey

For individual or group use.

£5.99 (plus p&p)

ISBN-10: 1-85345-312-9
ISBN-13: 978-1-85345-312-0

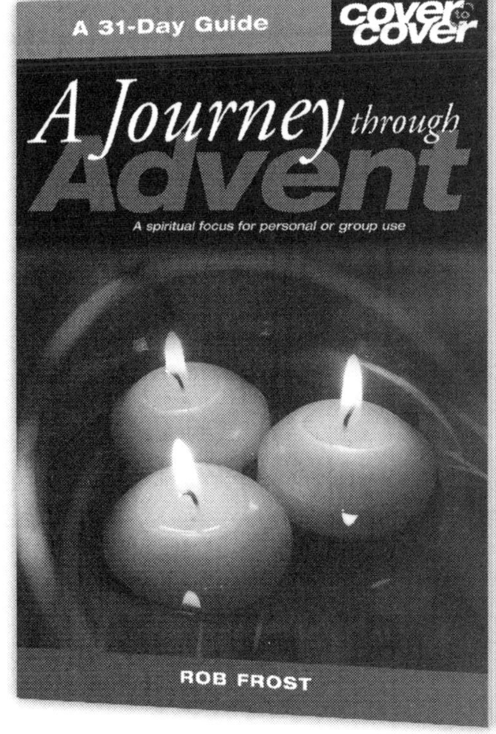

Prices correct at time of printing